Big Daddy Don Garlits Tales from the Drag Strip

Don Garlits

with

Bill Stephens

Foreword by Shirley Muldowney

Sports Publishing L.L.C.
www.sportspublishingllc.com

796.72
GAR

Director of production: Susan M. Moyer
Project manager: Jim Henehan
Dust jacket design: Kenneth J. O'Brien
Developmental editor: Elisa Bock Laird
Copy editor: Cynthia L. McNew
Photo editor: Erin Linden-Levy

All photos courtesy of the author.

ISBN: 1-58261-774-0

Printed in the United States of America

Sports Publishing L.L.C.
www.sportspublishingllc.com

CONTENTS

FOREWORD

If anyone has a few tales to tell, it's Big Daddy.
Many of them I'm familiar with (I'm sure a few of them involve me), but I doubt there are a whole lot of people who have heard many of the stories that Big Daddy has spun throughout this book. And let's face it, he's been around as long as drag racing has been around and in all those years has traveled to every corner of the racing world as a driver, innovator, and champion. And with almost each pass down the drag strip, another tale was born.

People give me credit for opening doors and becoming a pioneer, and that's nice. But if it weren't for Big Daddy, I don't think many of the racers who went on to become champions in this sport would have had the opportunities they had. He was always thinking two steps ahead of everyone else and took a great deal of satisfaction from out-thinking his competition as well as out-running them. He was sly, and still is, although the sport has changed so much in the last 40 years that money can sometimes make up for getting outfoxed by a crafty old master.

Big Daddy signed my competition license that helped to get me started in Top Fuel, and he probably thought at the time that I was just a novelty and I'd come to my senses before long. Well, that didn't happen, and now that I've retired I can take some pride in what my team and I have accomplished. Big Daddy and I had our share of struggles as we both pursued our racing careers, but we both experienced the excitement of winning races and winning championships, and that's what keeps people like us going. We've both been asked why we've drag raced for so long, and I think I can speak for the both of us when I say you never get tired of the rush of nailing that throttle, feeling the car shove your back into your seat, and getting to the finish line first.

That's what keeps you young!

Of course, when you think of Big Daddy, you think of what he has meant to this sport, especially Top Fuel, with his successful development of the rear-engined dragster. He and I both lost a few friends whom we raced against over the years because of terrible accidents involving those old front-engined cars, and I can only imagine how many of us are still around today thanks to Big Daddy. Not only did he revolutionize the cars we raced by making them safer, but he also made them quicker and faster. Every time you see Larry Dixon or Doug Kalitta or Brandon Bernstein rocket down the drag strip in four seconds at more than 330 mph, Big Daddy's incredible brainstorm has a lot to do with it.

Big Daddy is still out there, tinkering with his combinations, searching for more performance, trying out his latest ideas, and rolling up to the starting line at an age when most men are sitting on the porch playing checkers. He's a real, honest-to-goodness hero in the eyes of drag-racing fans around the world, and I'm pleased to say he's a gentleman and a friend. We didn't always get along, and we certainly had a few differences along the way, but I know we each respected each other. And *Tales from the Drag Strip* is the kind of book that will earn him a new generation of fans to go along with the many he already has.

There's only one Big Daddy: Don Garlits.

—*Shirley Muldowney*
Three-time NHRA Top Fuel champion

INTRODUCTION

The unshakable roots of NASCAR's stock car racing heritage were sunk deep into the fertile soil of the southern United States more than 50 years ago. What began as nothing more than a way for moonshiners and brawling roughnecks to bang and bash each other's fenders off on haphazard racetracks sketched out of muddy pastureland evolved into NASCAR racing and has grown to become a multimillion-dollar major league motorsport in only half a century. And even today, despite its more urbane pretensions, NASCAR has yet to completely shake its rebellious image as a product of the Confederacy.

How fitting is it, then, that the greatest drag racer of all time also hails from the Deep South.

"Big Daddy" Don Garlits and Top Fuel drag racing are about as synonymous as a proper name and a proper noun can become. The quotation marks that border his nickname are grammatically correct, but in the real world they are totally unnecessary. Big Daddy is a name that truly belongs to only one person, and he is far better known by it than by his birth name, Donald, which his parents, Edward and Helen Garlits, bestowed upon him on January 14, 1932.

As a young man who spent his formative years in the 1950s hot-rodding and street racing with a motley assortment of fellow motorheads in the Tampa area, Big Daddy was on his way to becoming the most notorious fuel racer in the country, and over the next six decades his quarter-mile adventures and exploits took on the size and scope of true American folklore—as quirky and colorful as any you'll find among NASCAR's most enduring legends.

Big Daddy didn't win the most drag races of anyone in the sport's history, nor did he win the most championships. It has been many years since he was the quickest or fastest Top Fuel driver in drag racing; in fact, it wasn't until 2001 that he made his first four-second run and clocked his first 300 mph speed. He is neither the wealthiest racer alive, nor the most flamboyant. But his legacy in the annals of high performance and organized drag racing is immense. He has achieved unmatched success as an innovator, pioneer, designer, visionary, free spirit, self-promoter, and relentless competitor—despite several near-fatal mishaps, which would have easily convinced a less-determined individual to call it quits.

In 2001, he was honored as the No. 1 racer on the National Hot Rod Association's list of the Top 50 Drivers of All Time as the NHRA celebrated its 50th anniversary. That fact alone shows the enormous respect that has been afforded him by the drag-racing establishment. He has had his share of differences with the NHRA and its founder, Wally Parks. Many of them have been well publicized, but both sides have readily come to admit that each has had a profound role in helping the other enjoy worldwide popularity and success.

As he moves into his seventies, Big Daddy is still as active, energetic, feisty, unchangeable, uncompromising, and morally grounded as he ever was, spending long hours watching over his beloved International Drag Racing Museum in Ocala, Florida, and making frequent appearances on a number of drag-racing and hot-rodding telecasts on ESPN and ESPN2.

This book is as close as many fans will ever get to sitting down with Big Daddy and listening to him weave the endless litany of personal experiences he has collected over the course of his fascinating life of unlimited speed. Here, in his own words, is a tasty collection of his most memorable tales, enthusiastically shared during hours of freewheeling conversations with the author, along with occasional assistance from Big Daddy's lovely wife, Pat, and his longtime friend and fellow racer, T.C. Lemons.

This is not Big Daddy's biography, but rather a random compilation of his favorite personal exploits, many of which still bring him genuine delight in the retelling and rarely fail to give him a chuckle as he recalls some of his most indelible memories. The names, dates, and places are accurate to the best of Big Daddy's remarkably acute pinpointing abilities, and the tales themselves are arranged in no particular order—much the same way as he related them during our conversations.

His life has been filled with triumph, tragedy, exhilaration, disappointment, success, and failure, but Big Daddy continues to soldier on at an age when most men are far beyond their prime. Slowing down isn't something

Big Daddy has had very much experience at, and after reading his *Tales from the Drag Strip*, you're sure to understand why.

Swamp Rat XVI is about to make its first pass in Amarillo, Texas, shortly after we finished the car. Note the lack of lateral struts on the wing. A few weeks later, the wing collapsed while I was making a run at Gainesville, and I almost crashed.

The Tales

B ig Daddy's first adventures in the hot-rodding universe unfolded, as they did for many post-World War II adolescents, from the heat generated by a relentless passion for automobiles. During the early 1950s, he and his buddies spent almost every waking hour working on their jalopies, racing them on Tampa's table-flat boulevards and side streets at night and devouring every shred of hot-rodding news and information presented in the various enthusiast publications that sprouted up, primarily, in Southern California.

As a teenager, with $345 that had taken him two years to scrape together, Big Daddy bought his first real car, a 1940 Ford Tudor, and was soon entrenching himself in hot-rod culture. His very existence was about to be directed by his unswerving desire to build and race fast cars, but little did he know how wild the journey would be.

IN THE BEGINNING

One of my first jobs when I was around 18 was working in the body shop at Ferman Chevrolet in Tampa, and that was where I first met Grady Pickle. Grady was a real hot-rodder, the first one I ever knew, and we just clicked. We became inseparable and were almost like shadows to each other.

He had a little red 1938 Ford convertible, and it really caught my eye the first time I saw it. You could take off the side panels below the hood on a 1938 Ford and look right down at the engine, and Grady's had a pair of Stromberg carburetors sitting on an Edmunds dual-intake manifold. To someone as green as I was when it came to hot-rodding, that was really impressive.

Now this was a pretty fast car. It had more than 100 horses, and 1938 Fords were fairly light cars, so Grady's could run a lot quicker than my 1940 Tudor, which was bigger and only had a stock, worn-out 85-horsepower engine in it. That's why I liked to ride with Grady when we went out at night.

One of the places where we used to race was over on Hillsborough Avenue, a four-lane road, around midnight. There were no cars around that late, and that's where you'd find the hot-rodders. We'd pull up to the traffic lights, and when they turned green, we'd hit the gas and take it up to third gear, which in those days was about 55 to 60 mph, and that would be the end of it—

Where it all began. I opened my dirt floor gas station in Tampa in the fall of 1956. This was the first step I took to make my interest in cars my livelihood.

just a little squirt. Grady's car would just pick off all of the other cars one by one, but on this particular night, we looked up and saw this little Ford roadster pull past and go up to the next light. I figured Grady could chalk up another victim, so I said, "Grady, get him!"

Grady looked back at me and said, "Noooo, I'm not racing that guy!" I couldn't believe it, because Grady was taking on everyone and beating them, so I asked him why not. He said, "That's King Hogan."

Well, Hogan had a 1927 T-roadster with a V-12 Lincoln engine. I still didn't know why that would cause a fuss with Grady until I remembered that we had gone to the races a few years earlier and King Hogan was the guy who won all of the time. He was the guy to beat, and Grady didn't want to race him.

We pulled up next to him at the light, and when it turned green, Grady just eased his car away and short-shifted his 1938. There was no way he was going to give King Hogan a run for it, so Hogan just gave us this little grin and tossed us a wave while he got on the gas and drove away.

BUBBA'S GIRL

It was quite an experience when I got my hands on my next car. One day Grady Pickle and I were riding around down on Waters Avenue, and I saw a black 1940 Ford convertible with a For Sale sign on it. I said, "Grady, quick…pull over in there!"

The lady who owned it wanted $550 for it, so I asked her if she'd take my 1940 Tudor in trade. She said she might know someone who would be interested in my car, and so she made a call to Bubba Hope. Bubba's younger brother, Dick Hope, was a pretty famous local race car driver who did pretty well, and Bubba had a used car lot, so they were always buying and selling cars.

Bubba came over and said he'd give me a $350 allowance for my car, which I turned over to this

woman. I actually made $5 on the deal since I had orig-
inally paid $345 for my car. Then I borrowed $200 from
my mother and bought the woman's convertible for the
$550 right on the spot.

It was so simple to buy a car in those days. I just
gave her the money and drove it away. She signed the
title and handed it to me; the tags stayed on it, there was
no insurance, and that was it.

About three weeks later I drove down to Sulphur
Springs and went past Bubba Hope's used car lot, and
there was my old 1940, sitting out there with $350 writ-
ten on the windshield. I went over and just started looking at it. Suddenly, Bubba came storming out to where
I was standing, and he started chewing on me about all
of the work he had to do to my 1940 and how he had
to replace the engine. Well, replacing an engine was
about a $40 deal in those days, and Bubba had gotten a
1948 Ford engine out of a wrecking yard and dropped it
in my 1940, which wasn't a big job.

Back then, used car lots had guys called *grease mon-
keys*, who were hired to scrounge up parts and then
repair the cars that the dealers took in, so it wasn't any
big deal. But Bubba was steamed up about having to
replace the engine.

When I thought about it afterward, it occurred to
me that it was pretty unusual for a dealer to come out
personally to look at a car being traded between private
parties and give a $350 allowance for a car that he was
going to sell for the same price. I finally realized that

Here I am at age 19 proudly posing with my 1940 Ford convertible. The year was 1951, and I consider this car my first hot rod.

Bubba and that lady had something going on that went a little further than trading used cars, which was fine with me because I came out of the deal in pretty good shape in the end.

There's more to the story. A couple of years later I ran into the guy who had owned that Ford convertible, and he was really upset that he had had to part with it. It turned out he had to give it to that woman because he had gotten her daughter pregnant! She took the car and used the money from the sale to take care of her daughter, who was sent up to Lake Ellen to have the baby before putting it up for adoption. There was no abortion in those days!

But that Ford was quite a hot rod. The fellow had just built a 1941 Mercury motor for it with the early Ford 85-horsepower crankshaft, which was a lot lighter than the original Mercury, and put in the 100-horsepower pistons. Man, let me tell you, it was a real rocket ship. It would just clean your plow!

Now I could outrun Grady!

FLATHEADS FOREVER?

The hot combination back in those days was the kind of setup I had in my 1940. If you had a six-cylinder engine of any kind, you weren't in the game. There were some 1949 and 1950 Cadillac and Oldsmobile V-8s available back then, but there wasn't any real speed equipment out there for them. They had hydraulic lifters, and they wouldn't rev up, but those flathead Fords had special heads and special camshafts. They had gone through some kind of development.

In fact, I once made the stupid statement, "Those overhead valve engines will never outrun these flatheads," but eventually, I was wrong on that one.

BEAT THE CLOCK

Just about the time I started getting more involved in racing, there was a base commander over at MacDill Air Force Base in Tampa who was a real hot-rodder. Over in the electronics shop at the base, he built a set of timing clocks, one for elapsed time through the quarter-mile and another for the 132-foot trap for top speed.

There was a perimeter road that ran behind the base; in fact, you can still see it today when you fly out of Tampa International Airport. It was too narrow for two cars to run together, but you could run one car down there without a problem. Well, once a month he'd set up the clocks out there and allow everyone to come out and run their cars to get a time. Now, back then most tracks only had guys using stopwatches to give you a time, and it was very rare that a track had a system that would give you your speed. You had to look down at your speedometer when you crossed the finish line, and that was how you determined how fast you were going. Most cars were running around 85 mph through the quarter at the time.

By then, we had been working on a flathead-powered coupe with an engine we had taken from a 1948 Ford coupe. We swapped a 331 cubic-inch early Chrysler Hemi into the coupe. We used it as a tow vehicle, because down in that area at that time if you were flat-towing your dragster and got behind some farmer on his tractor while you were on the way to or from the track, you needed some real power to pull out and get around him.

When we ran the dragster at MacDill that day we broke the transmission. Now in those days, races were really a family affair. People would bring their picnic lunches and make a day of it while racing their cars. There weren't any concession stands where you could buy your food or any other activities at these events, so if you weren't racing, there wasn't much you could do.

I told my wife, Pat, that because we couldn't run the dragster and we'd be hanging around all day, I wanted to take that 1939 coupe and see what it would run. The first thing she said was, "You'd better not break it, because if you do, we won't have any way to get home!"

Well, I decided to give it a try anyway. I eased it to the line, and with those old 8.20x15 treaded tires on it, I had to take it easy when I left and not break them loose. I got it right, and I went through the gears and shot down the track.

Now, our flathead dragster had made a full pass with a time of about 12 1/2 seconds at 108 mph. That coupe ran a 14-flat at 114 mph!

COUPE DE GRAS

On the way home after we ran our coupe in the drag race, I said to Pat, "Honey, the first guy to put one of those Chrysler Hemi engines in a dragster is going to be the guy to beat." And she said, "Well, you'd better put that one in your dragster right away!"

Big Daddy didn't need to be told twice.

Almost as soon as we got back, I dropped that Hemi into the dragster and couldn't wait to go up to Brooksville and see what we had. The engine still had the original ignition and a battery, it had dual-quads, and it went out and ran 10 1/2 seconds at 128 mph! I tell you what, the drag-racing world around here was set on its ear! That kind of performance had never been seen before. I mean, with the 12.5s we had been running, we were winning Top Eliminator!

There was this bike racer, Charlie Winslow, who raced a Harley on fuel called "Big Bertha," and it would run in the high 11s if he could get that thing hooked up. There was one time he beat us because we tore up the clutch before we knew to run a Velve-Touch clutch in the car, but after that, he never beat us again.

But after that big run we had in Brooksville, we flat-towed the dragster back home on one of those old, bumpy Florida two lanes, and by time we got back to Tampa, that frame in the dragster was sagging pretty good from the weight of that Chrysler engine.

This is the dragster that first bore the nickname "Swamp Rat," bestowed on it by Setto Postoian in 1956. This shot was taken in Kissimmee, Florida. Note the lack of any real driver protection and the hand-fabricated header pipes.

A CHEVY FROM THE LEVY

Soon thereafter, I went out looking for a frame for the Hemi-powered dragster. I was looking for a 1931 Chevy frame and found one in a junkyard on East Hillsborough Avenue. The reason I wanted a 1931 Chevy four-door frame is because the bodies had so much wood in them that they'd just rot away and you'd have the frame left over.

The fellow at the junkyard sold it to me for $50, but he told me I'd have to get the body off of it. I just pushed the whole thing over on its side, and that caused most of the rotted body to just fall off. Then I took a chisel and started banging all of the bolts and brackets off in no time. In fact, I got a real nasty cut from a rivet I got caught on, and I still have a scar from it on my hand that looks like a W. But the cut didn't slow me down a bit. I was anxious to get that frame back home and get a new car built.

EASTERN UPSTART

When we started running some impressive speeds down where we were, the California racers couldn't believe what we were doing. They thought we were getting the benefit of faulty clocks. Why shouldn't they think that? Here we were running 170 mph, and they were struggling to go 160. But they didn't understand the changes in the cars that had occurred. And it all started with an observation of mine: the importance of fuel volume.

Emery Cook had held the speed record at 168.22, and then the Speed Sport Roadster went 169 out in Arizona. But in 1957, we were watching the cars running at Cordova, Illinois, and it was interesting to see what was happening during the runs. Everyone ran Stromberg carburetors, and what you had to do was use a hand pump just before you launched to pump 10 pounds of pressure into the fuel system. That would sink the floats in the carburetors. There was a tube that ran up into the airhorn of the carburetors that created a low-pressure situation so that when the floats came back up during the run, extra fuel would go into the engine.

My first AHRA national event win was in this car in 1958 at Great Bend. The NHRA was still racing only gasoline. I also ran top speed in this car at Caddo Mills, Texas, hitting 168.22 mph.

At about the 1/8 mile, you could hear the engines run out of breath as the driver had to hand-pump the fuel pressure back up to 10 pounds for the rest of the run. I said to myself as I was watching this, "If they didn't do that in the middle, how fast would these damn things go?"

And I knew what was happening; they were running out of fuel. I even asked Cook what was going on, and he said, "Well, we're losing pressure, so I have to pump the pressure back up to get enough fuel into the carbs."

So I went home and ran a great big fuel line down to the tank into a great big two-by-two square fuel block with six lines going to six carbs, and when I had six pounds of pressure at the tank, I had six full pounds of fuel pressure right at the carburetors.

We got 176.40 mph in 8.79 seconds just like that. The Californians could believe it if they wanted to.

AND IF THEY DIDN'T...

In June 1958, three of the fastest cars from California all came out to Houston, Texas, to race me. Jack Ewell was there in Jim Kamboor's *Jado Special*, Pete Ogden was

I win top speed, low e.t., and Top Eliminator at Kissimmee, Florida, in 1956.

driving Romeo Palamides's real fancy-looking car, and Red Case had his little rear-engined dragster that was sponsored by Chet Herbert. They all lined up together on one side of the drag strip, and I was on the other. They raced me individually, one by one, and I outran them all and set top speed and low e.t.

Those boys went back to California, and all they could say was, "Well, shut my mouth…"

THE FIRST "BIG" WIN

I would like to think my first big win was the NHRA Drag Safari in 1955. That was a really big deal at the time. The NHRA went all over the country with their Drag Safari, and a lot of the racers followed them from place to place. When the Safari came down to Florida, a lot of the faster Eastern cars came down here to run in it. In 1955, there were 20 dragsters there.

Back then, after you outran all of the fuel dragsters, you had to outrun the gas dragsters. Then after your engine had been making all of those runs and getting tired, finally, you had to outrun the fuel coupes—all in the same day!

In those days, there was no qualifying. If 30 cars showed up, there were 15 pairs in the first round. If you were entered in the race, you were in the race. It didn't matter how many cars were there. And there was no eliminations ladder. You just ran your opponents based

Before moving permanently to Pomona, California, the NHRA's Winternationals were held in Daytona, Florida, in association with NASCAR. In the first year of the event, 1960, I won the biggest trophy for setting overall top speed for the five-day competition. Here I get a victory kiss from Miss Winternationals, Shelby Cardwell.

on who was next to you when you pulled into the staging lanes. The faster guys obviously wanted to race the slower guys, and there were times that there would be some sandbagging by the faster drivers, but that's the way it was done back then.

It didn't matter that year, because we outran everyone that day, and I still consider it my first big win.

THE CHALLENGES OF TRAVEL

You've got to remember that in the early days of drag racing, there were very few good, safe roads, and there were no interstates. Usually, in the very early days, the way that you towed your race car to the events was behind your passenger car with a tow bar, which was called *flat-towing*.

At the World Series in Cordova, Illinois, Dick Keller of *The Blue Flame* land speed car leans over the tire. We are changing the clutch. A short block is in the trunk of the 1955 Chevy.

I'll never forget one weekend down in Kissimmee; I made the mistake of letting one of the kids hook the tow bar up to the car, and he forgot to tighten up the hold-down on the hitch ball. So we were driving down U.S. 92, and I looked in the mirror. There wasn't a dragster back there any more!

It could have been a real disaster. That race car could have run into someone and killed them, but fortunately, when we turned around and went back, we got to the gate of the racetrack and saw that the dragster had come loose just as we were leaving and went straight into a ditch.

I am pushed along the return road at Cordova in 1957 in my Chrysler-powered dragster. That's Pat in the passenger's seat of the 1955 Chevy.

After that, I made a rule that from then on, I'd double-check all of the hookups myself.

LONG PULLS

It took a lot longer to get to and from the races years ago than it does now. In 1957, the first time we ever took a trip out of state, I believe the drive from Tampa

I towed my dragster out to the first U.S. Fuel & Gas Championships in California. The car in the background belonged to my West Coast rival Serop "Setto" Postoian. I still have the ram intake and carburetors in my museum. Note the spare engine ties to my trailer in the foreground.

to Cordova took about four days. We left in the middle of the day and took Highway 441 North all of the way.

It was the middle of the night when we got to Knoxville, and I could barely keep my eyes open, but I kept driving anyway. It's a wonder we didn't roll off a mountain somewhere. My stepfather and I had just built the trailer we were using, and we didn't know anything about wheel placement or anything like that. When we started climbing up those big hills and down those big grades with that race car swaying side to side behind us, it scared my wife nearly half to death!

Somehow, we made it to Cincinnati and visited Pat's uncle, who had a shop, and mounted some special shocks on the trailer to try to straighten it out. It helped a little, but what it really needed was to have the axle moved. Of course, we didn't know that at the time.

JU$TICE FOR ALL

We set out for Cordova after we left Cincinnati, and I remember thinking that the Sun tachometer I had on the dragster needed to be fixed. Sun's factory was in Chicago, so I figured we'd stop there on the way to the track and get it taken care of.

It was pretty early in the morning when we got to around Gary, Indiana, and the sky was sort of yellow from all of the steel mills out there. When we got to the eastern outskirts of Chicago, it was still morning and we had to drive to the other side of the city to where Sun was located. Well, we drove and we drove and we drove and it was way after dark. We still hadn't gotten there yet.

At some point we came to a set of traffic lights that turned yellow as we approached this intersection, and I kept going. The next thing I knew, a cop was pulling us over.

"Say, where ya headed, Sonny Boy?" he asked me.

"Oh, I'm from Florida, and we're going to that big drag race out in Cordova," I answered.

"Well, I don't know anything about that, but you went right through that traffic light back there," he continued.

"I know," I said, "but I thought it would be more dangerous to jam on the brakes than it was to keep going because it's late and there aren't many cars out."

"Ya know, rather than write you a ticket, there may be another way to take care of this whole issue," he offered.

Now down in Florida, you just didn't even try to make any kind of a deal with a policeman or you were going to find yourself in jail in no time. But this guy took me aside and said, "If you've got $10, we can settle this thing right here and I'll forget the ticket and you can just go right on."

"Are you serious?" I said with a look of disbelief.

"Oh yeah, I'm dead serious," he reassured me. "You give me the $10, and I'll forget the whole thing."

So I gave him the $10, and sure enough, I got into the car, drove away, and never heard another word about it.

BUT WAS IT WORTH IT?

The next morning we were at the Sun factory, and when I asked them about my broken tach, they said, "Fix a tach? Hey, we won't even sell you a tach! We have dealers for that!"

They didn't have a retail store there, and they didn't have a repair station. Nothing. That just goes to show you how naïve we were. We were just kids from Florida.

We had gone there for nothing. We just walked out and drove over to Cordova.

IN THE END, IT WAS

We had actually won the trip to Cordova by winning the most Top Eliminators down at Kissimmee with the ATAA (Automobile Timing Association of America). It was an all-expense paid trip, which amounted to about $400, and that was a lot of money at that time.

I was in the National Guard then, and my master sergeant was big into camping. He loaned us a big tent, and when we finally got to the track, we pitched it. We were in business.

But this was the race in Cordova where I had gotten the idea to get enough fuel pressure into the engine to keep it from bogging at the 1/8-mile mark. What a lot of people don't know is that I learned how to run my carburetors on 100 percent nitro that same weekend from Emery Cook.

I asked, "Mr. Cook, how do you get those carburetors to run on 100 percent? Because all I can get mine to take is 25 percent."

He said, "First, you get a gallon of nitro, add three ounces of 'Benny' to it, then you take the carburetors, drill out the dump tubes to 187-thousandths, throw the jets away, drill the needle and seat out to 120-thousandths, drill out the air bleeds to 60-thousandths, fix your pressure pump so it can run about six to eight pounds of pressure, get up to the line, pump it up to 10 pounds, let off the clutch, and take off. That's all there is to it."

My wife said, "Who's Benny?"

He said, "That's benzene, honey. If you need a gallon, you can have a gallon." And he reached over and gave us a gallon of it right off his truck.

I said to Pat, "We've gotta get out of here. We've got work to do!"

So we loaded the car on the trailer and drove over to the town of Cordova where there was a gas station. It was run by an old man, and his shop had two bays. I told him what I intended on doing—rebuilding my six carburetors—and I needed some power because I had to do some drilling. He let me get in there and get to work, and we didn't finish up until two o'clock the next morning.

We got back to the track after I made all of the changes, and it was race day. You could make all of the runs you wanted, and after we had made a couple of passes, we weren't running well at all. So I went over to Cook and said I had done everything the way he had told me, but the engine was missing and stumbling. He asked me how much fuel pressure I was running, and I said just a few pounds, which was whatever the fuel pump on the block was giving me. I didn't have a hand pump.

He said, "You have to have a hand pump. You need to pump that pressure up to 10 pounds."

Well, at this point we're about a half-hour before eliminations. Somebody said there was a guy back in the pits who had a hand pump he'd sell me, so I went around the pits looking for him. It turned out this fellow, Howard, who has been with Moroso for years, had a hand pump and sold it to me.

We took that pump, ran back to my car, took a screwdriver and chopped two holes in the cowl, ran a bolt up through there to hold the pump on, and Mickey-Moused some lines to hook it up into the pressure system. As soon as I was done, the guys running the show told me it was time to race Cook!

By 1958 at the age of 26, I had already won 300 races. Here I pose with just a few of my trophies.

Well, I got up there, and I've got pictures of me pumping away on that hand pump. Sure enough, we outran him—big time! I ran a 9.60, and it was the first time I had run in 9s.

When I came back down the return road, the fans went crazy because this wasn't some California guy who had run so quickly. They tore up their programs and threw the pieces out like confetti as I went past.

So I guess that first trip to Cordova was worthwhile after all. By the way, I still have the original carbs!

COOK-ED HIS OWN GOOSE

Emery Cook was the first driver to develop the high-gear-only concept back in the 1950s. He and Red Henslee were running their roadster at Santa Ana one day, and the two-speed Ford transmission they were using broke. When it got time for Top Eliminator, Cook said he didn't want to give up a shot at the trophy, plus a possible $25 for winning. He told Henslee, "Let's just go up there and run it in high gear, and maybe the other guy will leave too soon or break or who knows what."

Cook got up to the line, revved it up, and spun the tires, and sonavabitch, if he didn't set top speed of the meet and win! So they knew then that just running high gear could work.

The crowd was going crazy, and down at the far end, Henslee was so excited that he told Cook he wanted to be behind the wheel of the car as it was pushed back down the return road. But something goofy happened as they were coming back. They must have accidentally started it, and Henslee crashed.

Cook was so mad when Henslee crashed their roadster that the partnership was over for good.

166.97

Emery Cook and Cliff Bedwell, who had a body shop in San Diego, pooled their money and bought the Yeakel Cadillac dragster, which was a Scotty Fenn chassis with a Cadillac engine running on gas. They bought it without the engine because Cook was only interested in the chassis.

They worked up a high-gear shaft, dropped the Chrysler fuel motor in it that, I think, was the same motor from the Cook & Henslee roadster, and the following week went out to Long Beach. They went 166.97 mph. It was the first car over 160, a whole bunch over 160 at that.

And the following Monday, Wally Parks, the head of the NHRA, outlawed nitro.

HERO WORSHIP

Emery Cook was one of my early heroes. I hung on every word he said. Back when I spoke to him at Cordova in 1957, I called him Mr. Cook. He wasn't that much older than I was, but I respected him.

In my garage, I had a picture of that Cook & Bedwell dragster hanging up. Cook was like a guiding light for me.

Back in the 1960s I was campaigning my infamous Dodge Dart Funny Car roadster, driven by Emery Cook, who had been one of my early racing idols. This shot was from 1966.

ANOTHER COOK & GARLITS ADVENTURE

In 1965 we moved to Detroit—right next door to Dick Branstner, who had built a Dodge Dart for Jay Howell to drive. It was a white Dart, rear-engined, and had red, blue, and yellow dots all over it. It was called the *Polka Dart*.

They weren't doing much with it, because Branstner was big into Super Stocks. So Frank Wylie, the PR manager at Dodge, said to me, "We'd like you to go down the street and pick up that Dart and go run it."

I went down and said to Branstner, "They want me to come down here and pick up the *Polka Dart*." And that's what I did. The plan was to have Connie Swingle drive it and promote the whole thing with "Colorful Connie Swingle in the *Polka Dart*." We were going to paint the car all different colors, but the plan never materialized because Connie was too busy doing other things.

Emery Cook said he'd drive it.

We gave it a solid black paint job and finished it off real nice with "Garlits Dodge" painted on the side. We towed it over to the Detroit Dragway for its maiden voyage. Cook made the first pass, everything went pretty well, and we decided we were going to step on it a little bit. On the next run, I looked down the track, and I couldn't believe my eyes. The Dart was pointing right for the sky! The car was flipping over backward, the engine over-revved, the clutch came out of it in a thousand pieces, and finally Cook climbed out OK. This was in the afternoon and there were no people there, so nobody got hurt.

But here's the funniest part of the story. We didn't know it at the time, but a piece of the clutch flew up and took a chunk out of the track's power line, not enough to snap the line but just enough to weaken it. That night, I had a match race there in my Top Fuel dragster against Connie Kalitta, and that was a pretty big show.

We raced once to begin the show before the lights came on, and everything was fine. I won that one, and later on, we came to the line for the next race, but now it was dark. They turned the lights on, and everything seemed normal, but just as our cars were hitting the finish line, everything went black!

Now the Detroit Dragway had ditches on either side of the track, and there were these muddy gullies from erosion that lined the drag strip. This was one place where you didn't want to drive off the asphalt. Suddenly, it was totally dark, and to say our rear ends were pinching O-rings would have been an understatement.

Luckily, I remembered that the Ford plant that was off in the distance was right in line with the racetrack, so I saw the gas pipe with the flame on top that stood up over the factory and just steered for that. I kept the clutch out so the engine would help back me down, and I got the car stopped, all of the while waiting for Kalitta to run over me!

Kalitta was somehow able to stop without a problem, and when we got out of our cars, I walked over and asked him if he had steered for the flame, too. He said, "The only flames I saw were the ones coming from your exhaust pipes, and I just followed them. I was hoping you knew where you were going, 'cause, Big Daddy, that's where I was going!"

SHADES OF CHESTER, SOUTH CAROLINA

My crew and I made the trip up to Chester, South Carolina, but Pat decided to stay home. On my first run, I went 177 mph, and we were trying to go 180. We went back and poured a bit more nitro into the tank. We figured the extra load would get us the 180 we were looking for.

So on the next run I got it down through there and everything was fine, but I made a mistake. Of course, back then I didn't know it was a mistake. You know how when you coast down a hill, take your foot off the gas, and turn off the ignition, it helps cool your engine? Well, I figured when I let my foot off the throttle at the end of the run, I'd turn off the ignition and help cool the engine, because we were running some pretty high temperatures in the engines back then.

Today, we know you can't do that; in fact, that's why we don't have rev-limiters on nitro engines. When I let my foot off and touched the magneto kill switch, it blew the blower, and suddenly I was engulfed in flames!

I had never felt heat like that in my life. I wasn't wearing any real fire protection because we never had had fires in those cars. I did have on a helmet, but I wasn't wearing gloves or a fireproof mask. I was wearing a leather jacket that Pat had given me before I left Tampa. She gave it to me because at the time, we were driving in short-sleeved T-shirts, and she was concerned that if I ever flipped, I'd get scraped up pretty bad without something covering my arms.

When that fire hit me, I thought it was all over. My life was flashing before my eyes, and I was drifting into unconsciousness. Time is a strange thing. You'd be surprised how much you can see in what, in reality, is only a few seconds.

Somehow I got the car stopped, and the fire went out. The fresh air hit me, and it woke me up a bit. I was able to get out of the car, and when I did, I looked down and the flesh was literally hanging off my hands. The pain was excruciating. My first thoughts were how burns were so dangerous and that it took forever for them to heal. I felt I might not make it.

I was taken to a little country hospital, and I called Pat. I told her I was mixing fuel in the pits and had a little flash fire, so she should come up to Chester because I might be there a couple of days. She was pregnant with our first child, and I was concerned about how she would handle this.

When Pat got to the hospital, she wasn't really expecting anything bad. Out in the hallway, the nurse told her that if I made it through the next 72 hours, I'd have a chance! When she walked into the room, I was all bandaged up and my nose looked exactly like a burned-up marshmallow. That was a shock for her.

Two or three weeks later, my mother came up to see me, and I was still pretty rough. The doctor came into my room and told me that he wanted to amputate the hand I'd had on the brake handle. It had been burned right to the bare bone, and he felt he had to take it off. I told him, "No, you can't take my hand off. I'd rather die."

He went to my mother and Pat and wanted them to sign the release to perform the surgery, but they wouldn't do it. They told him, "It's up to him."

The doctor said, "If I can't remove that hand, I think you need to go to another hospital, because if you get gangrene, it's all over, and I don't want you dying while you're under my care."

Pat called around and found that Tampa General Hospital had a burn specialist. He said, "Sure, bring him on down and we'll take him and let him die here comfortably."

So we took a train down to Tampa, and all of the while I was in unbelievable pain. My brother met us at the train station, and I must have weighed about 80 pounds. I was just skin and bones. Somehow, I was still able to walk.

The doctor, his name was Cullen, met me at the hospital, and by then, my hands were beginning to web and curl over; in fact, I think that other doctor wanted to take off both my hands. He hadn't thought either one of them was ever going to work again. But Dr. Cullen, I'll never forget, took my hands in his and just like that, he pulled them out straight and it was like they just burst at the seams. He said, "We've got to get you right up to surgery!"

Now this was with no prep or anything like that. One minute I was on the examination table, and the next, I'm in surgery. I was lying there and they were fixin' to plug the sodium pentathal into me when the doctor walked in wearing his white scrub suit.

I'll never forget this. He stood over me and put his hands on each side of my face. They were shaking like a leaf! I said, "Doc, what's wrong?!" He said, "Well, I've done 5,000 sets of hands of young men who were burned in tanks in Korea, and I get like this, but I'll be all right in just a minute."

And he reached up into this cabinet where he had a fifth of Wild Turkey, and he proceeded to take a big shot of it right out of the bottle! Almost immediately, his hands got nice and steady. They shot me up with the sodium pentathal, and the next thing I knew, I woke up and it was all over.

The recovery period was long, and there was a lot of pain. I literally had to keep my hands in saline solution around the clock every day. They had a pan that was filled with the solution, and I had to sit up with my hands in that solution until finally all of the raw tissue began to heal over.

Dr. Cullen was a miracle worker. When you look at my hands today, you can hardly tell that they had ever been burned. I've never had plastic surgery on them, and that doctor back in Chester wanted to cut them off! But I was serious about not letting him do it. I'd rather have died than not to be able to work with my hands.

ART MALONE'S TIMELY VISIT

W hile I was in the hospital, I had already announced I was through. I was quitting. I had talked to my brother, Eddie, and he had started selling off some of our engines and parts.

One day, Art Malone came up to visit with his wife and said he wanted to drive my car.

Art Malone has been both a great friend and racing rival. Here he congratulates me after losing in the final round of the 1961 *Drag News* 1320 Challenge at Golden Triangle.

Now, I still had a few bookings and some of them were pretty lucrative, $450 to $500, which was a lot of money back then. He said he'd drive it for 40 percent of the gross, which I had come to discover was pretty much most of what we'd be left with after expenses, but I said OK anyway.

So I took him over to Kissimmee. He made a couple of squirts, and it was like a duck taking to water! Then I took him to his first race up at Sanford, Maine, and right out of the trailer he goes 183.66 and breaks my world record of 182.54 that I set in Houston the week before Chester!

Now Setto Postoian was a Midwest racer who really worked me over after that. He was one of those guys who never believed the elapsed times and speeds I had run, and now he went wild when Malone broke the record.

One minute I was burned and it was all over, and the next, I was back with this kid and he was better than I was. And that's where the name "Swamp Rat" came from. Setto put this half-page ad in *Drag News* that said, "You're nothing but a 'swamp rat' because you're only in this sport to see what you can get. You shoot your mouth off about safety, and you put a green kid in a Top Fuel dragster with no experience and send him down through there."

Now, Malone in the meantime had gone 190 mph in nine seconds at Dunkirk, but that was on one of those old timing systems where you ran over the rubber hose, and we knew that wasn't accurate. But he set the elapsed time record at Great Bend with 8.26 at 178, and Setto wrote in a subsequent column, "You went 190 in 9 seconds at Dunkirk, but 178 at 8.26 in Great Bend. Explain it, pal!"

Well, we know now that those numbers were possible, but back then, we thought when you had a big speed, you had to have a quick e.t., too. The upshot of all of this was that Setto was beating the drum to get us some match races, and I'll tell you, it really worked. The phone rang off the hook. We were getting calls for us to race Setto everywhere.

You want to know what the funniest thing was? Setto never made it to the races! We'd get to the track, and there was no Setto! He could never get there! Something unexpected always happened that kept him from showing up!

DECEMBER 1959

It was announced that there was going to be a big East-West Challenge at the Riverside Raceway out in California, and every big-name Top Fuel car was going to be there, including Art Chrisman, who had just gone 181 mph. Of course, that was a "real" speed because it happened out in California and all of our times were phony, right?

Art Malone and I decided we were going out there, and the event was going to be held on the Sunday before Christmas. We drove out there in my 1950 Cadillac four-door and pulled an open trailer with *Swamp Rat I* sitting on it. Setto Postoian was supposed to be there because *Drag News* was really promoting the heck out of this race, and they printed a big map in one of their issues showing all of the states where all of these Top Fuel cars were coming from for this big meet at Riverside.

When we got there, we could see all of the fast California teams had shown up, including the "Speed Sport" guys and a bunch more. When we got to eliminations, Malone was running steady 8.50s one after the other at 181 or 182 mph. He was just picking cars off one by one, and they orchestrated it so Malone would have to face Chrisman in the final—and Malone outran him, too.

And the story that ran in the next *Drag News* had the headline, "The 'Rat' Took the Cheese!"

A LITTLE HELP
FROM HIS FRIENDS

While we were running that day out in Riverside, the Cadillac broke its fuel pump. There was another West Coast racer/cam grinder there who came over and fixed it for us between rounds, and back then it wasn't like it is today. We only had about 20 minutes between rounds, but he came over and took care of it for us anyway. That man was Ed Iskendarian.

After the race we went to collect the prize money, and because my deal was for a percentage of the gate, we walked out of there that day with $7,000! It was a few days before Christmas, and we wanted to get back home for the holiday, so we packed up. Someone asked me, "Garlits, where are you headed?" And I told him we were driving straight through to Florida. He said, "Well, that's a really long pull. Have you got anything to help you stay awake?" I told him I didn't, and he took out some pills and said, "Here, if you take one of these, there's no way you'll fall asleep." He called the big black pill a *Los Angeles Turn-Around*, meaning you could take this pill and drive to Los Angeles and back to Florida without sleep!

So I took that pill, and we got out on the road. Art Malone was asleep in the back seat, and all of a sudden around Phoenix, I yelled out "Malone! Malone! Wake up!"

He jumped up and asked me, "What's wrong?"

I shouted back, "Look at that big elephant right in the middle of the road!"

I guess that pill I had taken was giving me hallucinations. So Malone said, "I'll drive!" and I got into the back seat and went to sleep. I never woke up until we hit the Florida state line.

CHRISTMAS BONUS

We made it back home in time for Christmas, and this will show you how we raced in those days. I think Christmas that year was in the middle of the week, and the following weekend, there was the big South Florida Timing Association Gas Championships down in Miami. It paid $500 to the winner. Art Malone said to me, "Hey, let's take the car down to Miami and win that $500!"

Well, the race in Miami was for gas dragsters, and we had to convert over our fuel motor to run gasoline for this event. So we took the nitro fuel pump off and put the gas fuel pump on, put gasoline nozzles in the injectors, put the car on a trailer, and went down there. We just cleaned their plows, took the money, and came right home!

We never even took the heads off that motor between Riverside and Miami. We looked at the rod bearings after we won at Riverside, and we hadn't even hurt them. And this was what was called a *welded stroker*, which had a welded crankshaft with a longer stroke. They didn't always last a long time. Sure enough, after Miami our luck ran out.

My brother, Ed, sits in *Swamp Rat I* as we warm up the car during the 1958 World Series of Drag Racing in Cordova, Illinois. I (center) supervise. I won the event that weekend but a year later was badly burned in an accident.

BAD RUN OF LUCK?

We had a deal to go run up in Biloxi, but at the time, we didn't know diddly about crankshafts breaking. We found out soon enough. Art Malone was on this run at Biloxi and was really flying down through there when there was this huge "BOOM!" The engine blew up. I had a picture of that explosion for years, and the engine finally went up because the crankshaft broke in four or five places!

I had put that engine in the car right after Bakersfield in March 1959, and we ran it all year. It wasn't until the following year, in the spring of 1960, that it finally blew up. You couldn't dream of doing anything like that today.

We were paying Malone 40 percent of the gross, so we were actually struggling to stay out there. We didn't have a lot of money for the engine and parts, and I still had some races to go to. Up until then, I had no idea a stock 392 Hemi could make enough power to run fast, because we were used to running strokers. Because we couldn't afford to get another stroker motor, I did the only thing I could do. I got a stock 392 cubic-inch Hemi and put forged racing pistons in it with aluminum rods. Man, if that engine didn't have that car running like a rocket ship! It was a short stroke, so it picked up the boost, and it was a more efficient engine.

We never ran a stroker again.

BIG DADDY BURNS AGAIN

One time Connie Swingle and I were out at Golden Triangle testing in the middle of the week. I was part owner of the track; in fact it was two other partners, Jim Kaylor and Jimmy Diez, and me who built the track, so I could test whenever I wanted.

We had been working at the shop building *Swamp Rat III*, which was almost finished, but we were out testing *Swamp Rat I* on this particular afternoon, getting ready for a match race against Art Malone coming up in Detroit. I was making a run when the engine kicked out a rod. I wasn't running any water in the block, just "Rock Block," and oh, what a fire I had. But at least this time, I was wearing some protection. Not a lot, but some.

Up top I had on a mask and my jacket, so that was fine. But I had on blue jeans tucked into my socks, and they were burned away completely right down to my bare skin. I had some really bad burns on my legs. There was a fellow, George Roberts, with me that weekend, and believe it or not, he had been talking to me back then about making a drag-racing movie. He was a big movie buff, and he had plans for shooting this big movie about what we were doing. It never materialized, but I was glad he was there that day.

He and the guys got me into our station wagon, drove me home, which was quite a few miles, and went in and told Pat that I had been burned pretty badly and that I should be taken to the hospital.

We got to the hospital, and they checked me right in and began treating the burns. The next morning when the doctor came to my room, I had my clothes on, and he said, "Where are you going?" I said, "I'm going home! I've got work to do, and you've got me all bandaged up, so that's about all you can do for me, right?"

He said, "Hey, I'm not going to be responsible for you if you go home. I need you here in the hospital." I told him, "Doc, you ain't gonna be responsible for me no matter where I am. I'm going home where I can work with my hands, because they're fine. I just have to be careful with my legs, but I'll be better off at home and I can heal up and get better. I'll check in with you once a week, and I'll be OK."

I also didn't want to take any pain medication. Nothing. Zero. I just wanted to go home, and so I did. I had had some burns that were a lot worse, so I knew something about them. I knew I'd heal up just fine.

SWINGLE PINCH HITS

I couldn't drive the match race with Art Malone in Detroit, but Connie Swingle went up there after we threw some black paint on *Swamp Rat III* and did pretty well. He won one of those rounds against Malone, which was really good because Art was a killer. He had his new car, and he was tough. But *Swamp Rat III* ran strong right away, and that made us happy.

I decided to let Swingle drive the car to honor the contracts we had for the rest of the year, and I took some time to heal up. I became more of a crew chief for a while.

Swamp Rat III, the car that made the sport's first seven-second run, a 7.88, with Connie Swingle driving in 1968.

RACING AS A BUSINESS?

Racing wasn't our sole source of income back in the 1960s when we were traveling around the country. We always had our speed shop at 12200 Nebraska Avenue, and that provided a lot of our income, too. In fact, had you asked me then, I really didn't think you would ever be able to make a living drag racing. I never thought drag racing would grow to the size that it is. I figured it would remain more an amateur sport because there were so many participants. We really liked it the way it was, because anybody could race then that wanted to.

In NASCAR, you had only a select number of drivers, but in drag racing, we sort of shared the glory with Gas Coupes and Sedans, Gas Dragsters and the Roadsters. We shared the facility, and we competed for the attention of the fans from within the sport.

Another of the great match races between Tommy Ivo and me. This one is at Bud Creek, Maryland, on July 21, 1963. I won the best two of three rounds by taking the first two runs. This was the clincher with *Swamp Rat V* running a 7.91-second pass at 191.26 mph to Ivo's 8.01-second run at 192.70 mph.

After I sold *Swamp Rat 2-B* to local racer Jim Kaylor, the car was fitted with two small-block Chevy engines. Here it is at the Tampa Dragway in 1963.

But that's always been OK with me, because I didn't get into racing like it was NASCAR or IndyCar and there was a lot of money at stake. I got into it because I liked the sport. Now, there are professionals and sportsmen racers. Drag racing was structured that way when I got into it, and it's still structured that way now. Some people have stated they'd like to see it become all professional. I think that the pros should be separated from the sportsmen classes today. That would give both classes equal publicity at their championship events. However, the fact of the matter is I've seen some things since I had the museum that I didn't know before. The sportsmen are the backbone of the sport. They pay the bills and they buy the parts; they're the ones who pay the admission to the museum—not the pros. They all get in for free! When we have a big race at Moroso or Bradenton, we can count on all of the sportsmen racers to show up and put money in the turnstiles.

I'm thankful for that, and I would never want to come out and say we should eliminate those sportsman classes because we don't need 'em any more. As far as I'm concerned, we still need 'em. Hey, that's how I started. I was a sportsman racer. That's all there was. That was drag racing.

SUPER STOCK DODGE

In the fall of 1961, Chrysler had me come up to Detroit and showed me the 1962 Super Stock Dodge. They said they wanted me to have one. It had a 413 wedge-head engine and a cross-ram intake manifold—it was a trick car.

I'll never forget I took delivery of that car and it had a 3:31 rear axle in it. The first big race where all of the Super Stocks would be showing up was going to be at Green Valley in Texas. So my wife and I packed up our suitcases, threw them in that Dodge, and drove it to Green Valley! When we got to Texas, we went to a

Dodge dealer and had them put a 4:56 rear end in it. We drove it to the race, ran it, came back to the dealer after the race, and had them put the 3:31 back in it. We drove all of the way home to Tampa. It was really a stock car! And it was a fast car! It ran 13.5 or 13.6 at 112 mph. I ran it all year, and then in 1963, I got a new lightweight car.

Here's a story about what happened with that 1962 car that was pretty funny. First of all, Pat and I were driving out to Texas, just cruising along the highway. Now, nobody knew anything about these 413 cars then. They only built about 13 of those Dodges. They didn't have any badges, any decals or anything like that. It just looked like a red Dodge sedan.

Anyway, Pat and I are driving to Texas on one of those long, straight stretches down there and I looked in the mirror. I saw this Ford, I think it was a "high-riser," coming up on me. He pulled up beside me and slowed down to my speed, about 80 or so. I stepped on it a little and got up to 90, and the Ford was right there. I got up to about 100, and the Ford was right there. Next thing we knew, we were running around 120 mph.

I had a 3:31 gear, remember. The Ford was just about to run out of breath. The Dodge had those two big dual quads on a cross-ram, and when I stepped all of the way down on it, I couldn't believe I had been only running about half throttle! When I put it to the wood, I looked in the mirror and saw two thick black tire marks on the highway behind me! With a 3:31 gear, that

Dodge is leaving rubber at 120 mph and we just drove away from that Ford! I bet that guy talks about that to this day to his grandchildren!

Now, that Ford must have been a powerful one, because he was doing all right up until 120. Then it was all over.

The 1962 Dodge in my museum is actually a replica of the one I had. The original Dodge I raced is in some dentist's garage somewhere in the Southeast, exactly the way it was when I raced it—and the guy won't give it up! It's probably worth a couple of hundred grand!

This car was kind of a one-off. It didn't look like a 1961, and it didn't look like a 1963. So if you try to

Here I am behind the wheel of my 1962 Dodge hardtop with a 413 cubic-inch Max Wedge engine, one of only 13 1962 Dodges ever built with that motor. I raced it in the Super Stock class until I began devoting all of my time to dragsters.

restore one, you've got a problem because you can't swap many parts with it.

Luckily, we found a real dry 1962 not too long ago that came with a 318 and got our hands on it. We replicated my car, because I knew what they had done at the factory when they put the 413 in it. I knew where the holes needed to be drilled and where everything went, and it came out real nice. It looks great in the museum. Nicer than my original car, in fact, because we beat that one to hell and back!

"COLLECTING" THE CASH

When we got to the track in Green Valley, Bill "Maverick" Golden and Tommy Grove were both there, two guys who had some experience racing Mopars. It was the first time I had ever seen either of them.

Tommy had made his own special set of collector-style, fender-well headers that siphoned the cylinders just right, and I believe he won the race that weekend. He was really fast. Well, I couldn't wait to get home and build my own set of fender-well headers. Right as I began to build those headers, who walks through the door but Connie Swingle. So I got him building those headers and I hired two more guys to help. Those headers were as good as any out there. We'd build a set of headers, which sold for about $40, put them in a burlap bag, take them down to the bus station, and ship them out all over the country, and I tell you we were making some money.

PASS THE NITRO

We raced another Dodge, a special lightweight car with a 426 Max Wedge engine and aluminum front end and aluminum doors, for about six months in 1963. But then, we were really into the dragster because I had won the Winternationals in 1963 with *Swamp Rat 5-A*. That car was a little too light and short, so we built *Swamp Rat 5-B*. My wife and I went on tour with it, towing it with a 1963 Dodge station wagon with an enclosed trailer that Pete Robinson built for us. A lot of

This was my first pass at more than 200 mph. The place was Bainbridge, Georgia, and the year was 1960.

people don't know that Pete was in the trailer business for a while.

The next trailer we designed ourselves. It had an angle iron frame and plywood sides that were bolted on for strength. It's the way they build 18-wheeler trailers today, with plastic sides all bolted and riveted in. That's what gives them their strength.

I was really busy with the dragster and wasn't able to devote my full attention to the Super Stocker. It was out touring, but I had other drivers racing it for me. Then my boss at Chrysler got mad at me and said I wasn't driving the car enough. He called me and said, "We want you to turn it in!"

I went down to Massey Motors in Tampa and turned it in. I don't know where that car went, but I was out of the Super Stock business.

It was actually OK with me, because I couldn't really make any show money with the Super Stocker. We were racing it all around the southeastern United States, but it only paid around $200 to $300 to show up. By then I was making around $750 to $800 show money with the fuel dragster. And a lot of people don't know it didn't cost any more to run the fuel dragster than it did to run the Super Stocker. Nitro was only $1.40 a gallon, and you only used a gallon or so on a run. And there was no mechanical attrition. You didn't have to take the heads off the nitro motor after every run.

You actually worked harder on the Super Stocker than the dragster! Every time you ran the Super Stocker,

I set a new all-time speed record, 186.32, at the Detroit Dragway in 1960. That's a member of my crew, Leslie Lemme, kneeling in the foreground and carefully watching the run. Note the traffic light-style Christmas Tree that hung over the starting line.

you had to come back, pull the heads off, make sure the valves were perfect because you were running those little 1/16-inch valve seats that were all angled, and everything had to be just right. We could run things a lot more raggedy in the nitro motors.

Monetarily and publicity-wise, it made more sense to be in the nitro cars. Chrysler didn't stop supporting me at that point; they just wanted me to turn in the Super Stocker so that somebody else could go out and race it. Besides, they had just introduced the 426 Hemi, and they wanted me to do a lot of development work with that engine for Top Fuel.

CHRYSLER COMES A-CALLIN'

When we started working with the new Hemi, we had our Super Stocker out there running, we had my fuel dragster out there running, plus Connie Swingle and Marvin Schwartz were out there with fuel cars. Swingle had a 426 in his car, and Marvin had a 392. So we had the *Garlits Chassis Special*, *Swamp Rat VIII*, the *Wynn's Jammer*, and the Dodge sedan.

Plus, my brother, Ed, was running the *Swamp Rat 2-C*, which was a blown 392 burning gasoline. It was a good-running car. Back at Green Valley in 1961, he won the Gas Dragster class, and back in those days, they ran the Gas winner against the Fuel winner to determine the overall Top Eliminator. Ed raced Zane Schubert in that final and just got beat by that fuel car in a really close race. And a lot of people don't know that it was back in 1958 when we were running gasoline that my relationship with Chrysler really began.

We had had several versions of *Swamp Rat 2*. The first one was what we called the *Banana Car* because we built the chassis out of EMT tubing, and when we came back from Miami after running it down there, the chassis was drooping like a banana. So we built a chassis out of square tubing and put a Buick engine in it, and it ran really well for a long time.

Well, Howard Johansen built the first set of aluminum heads for a small-block Chevy, which a lot of people don't know, and he gave them to me. So we built a small-block Chevy, a stroker motor, put the aluminum heads on it, took the Buick engine out of *Swamp Rat 2*, put the Chevy in the square tubing frame, and took it up to Brooksville. It ran pretty well—10.5 at about 140. Boy, I'll tell you, word about that spread around quickly.

We began to think about running fuel in that engine, because with the aluminum heads, we could run a lot of nitro through that Chevy. Then one day, I got a call from Chrysler.

Now, this was 1958. I had no relationship whatsoever with Chrysler. I was buying my engines in the junkyard. This fellow from Chrysler says, "We understand you ran a Chevy in your dragster."

I said, "Well, yes, I did."

He says, "Well, we don't like that. What's wrong with the Chrysler?"

I said, "It's something we do. Ya know, we're always experimenting with different things to see what we can develop."

And he says to me, "We'd be more comfortable if you'd take that Chevy engine out and put a Hemi back in that car."

I said, "Well, I had a Buick in there before."

"But you can drop a Hemi in there, can't you?"

"Yeah," I said, "I can do that."

He finally says, "Then we'd be happy to supply you with some engines if you can do that."

Now, here's what they did from then on. There were a lot of these wealthy guys who bought Chrysler 300s and ran 'em hard and put 'em away wet. These were good customers of Chrysler, and the engines were under guarantee. These owners would beat these cars until something broke, like a rod bearing or something like that, and they'd drive them back to the dealer and shout, "Hey, my engine blew up!"

Chrysler would drop a nice new engine—a new short-block assembly—into their cars, make them happy, and send the old engines to me.

On December 14, 1958, I smoked my way to 8.6 seconds at more than 180 mph in Brooksville, Florida. Note the lack of guard rails or barriers between the strip and spectators.

It was perfect for me, because we had to grind the cranks anyway, and the engines were in pretty good shape otherwise. So after that, I got all of the 392 Hemis I ever wanted from Chrysler. That was the beginning of our relationship.

HEMI STYLE

Now, there's more to the story concerning my trip to Detroit in 1961 to see the 413 Dodge. I was at Chrysler with Lou Furlong and Dick Landy, and we were getting the "big tour." They showed us the Super Stockers, but a lot of people don't know this.

They took us to the Chrysler Hemi engine plant, and remember they were building the Hemi right from the moment they started building the wedge-head engines in 1959. The assembly line for the Hemi was right alongside the assembly line for the wedge engines. They were even still building a few 354 Hemi engines for marine and industrial use, and here's the part you probably didn't know. They had these banks of dynos at the plant, and every early model Hemi that they built was put on the dyno and run in. Then they pulled the oil pan, checked the bearings, figured out just how much horsepower each engine had, sealed it back up, and then dropped it into the cars on the assembly line or shipped it to wherever it was going.

Those were the days!

A LEGEND HELPS
A LEGEND-TO-BE

When I first started running those Chrysler engines, I was having a problem with spun bearings. I knew that Lee Petty was running those engines in NASCAR and had won down in Daytona in 1954. I remembered he lived up in North Carolina in this little town called Level Cross, so I thought I'd call him up and ask him if there was something I could do to fix the problem.

They had operators back then, and when I called the one in Level Cross, I asked her if she had a number for Lee Petty. She said that he didn't have a number and that she'd have to ring over there for me. So she did, and Lee Petty himself answered the phone.

I said, "Mr. Petty, this is Don Garlits, and I run an engine just like the one that you won Daytona with, but I'm having trouble with it and I need some help."

He said, "What kind of trouble are you having?"

I said, "I can't keep the bearings in it."

He said, "Have you got a pencil?"

"I sure do."

He said, "Write these numbers down."

He gave me the numbers I needed for turning down the crank and how much to hone out of the cylinders. Then he told me I had to go get some 60-weight airplane oil and put that in there and I wouldn't have any more trouble. I went back and did everything he told me to do, and, sure enough, I never had any more trouble!

Two months before Lee Petty died, Pat and I were driving down Interstate 220 and we saw a sign that said, "Level Cross." I said, "Let's go over and see what the Pettys' place looks like." It was a Sunday, and when we got there, the museum was closed, but up on the hill was the big white house they live in. I walked up there and knocked on the door. Who should answer the door but Lee Petty himself!

He said, "Don Garlits, what in the world are you doing in Level Cross?"

I said, "Well, we were driving past and saw the sign for Level Cross and wondered if any of the Pettys were home."

And he said, "Why don't you just come on in here and sit a spell? We'll drink a glass of iced tea and talk about racing."

I got to sit there and talk to him for about three hours, and I really enjoyed it. It was just so wonderful. And then not long thereafter, he died.

And he made such a strong impression on me back in 1954 when he took my phone call and helped me that I try to do the same thing when someone comes to me for some help with their car. It's because I remember Lee Petty, the Daytona winner, took the time to help Don Garlits when I was really a "nobody."

TWO "KINGS" ARE BUNK-MATES IN VIETNAM

Back during the Vietnam War, President Nixon asked a bunch of racers around December if they'd go over to Vietnam and visit some of the kids who were fighting and weren't going to make it home for Christmas. So I spent 16 days rooming with Richard

In 1971 I made a visit to Vietnam on behalf of the U.S. government. Back row (left to right): Ray Marquette, Art Pollard, General Yeo Abrams, Richard Petty, Butch Hartman, and Captain Fettis. Front row: Wally Dallenbach Sr. and me.

Petty in Saigon. I'll tell you, it was something I'll never forget when we had to helicopter out to where the troops were in the field.

We took fire as we flew over the jungles, and we returned machine gun fire with the Viet Cong. Luckily, we were flying high enough that they couldn't hit us, but we could hit them.

But the time I spent with Richard showed me he is a real person. What you see is what you get. And I know it was devastating when his grandson, Adam, was killed a few years ago. He was really close to him, and I don't think the family has recovered from it yet.

TRICKS OF THE TRADE

There were some things that we did every so often to help give us an advantage if we thought we needed one.

For instance, if we were going to run somebody who was really tough and the race was probably going to be decided by who left the line first, it wasn't unusual for us to take some STP or another oil treatment like Charge and put a little down in one of the exhaust pipes. That stuff is real thick and gooey, so when you start the engine, everything is fine and there's nothing unusual happening. But when that engine heats up and that exhaust pipe gets hot, there's a puff of blue smoke out of that pipe on every exhaust pulse.

I prepare for a match race against my good friend, Chris "The Greek" Karamesines at Milan, Michigan, in 1967. The car was the newly rebuilt *Swamp Rat II.* I inadvertently insulted Karamesines when I told him, "I didn't really build it for racing you."

Now what happens is that your opponent looks over and thinks you've got a cylinder out, and it throws them off their game plan a little bit. So they don't "push the light" as hard because they don't want to risk a redlight against a car they think has a problem, and that gives you an advantage. I've done it lots of times.

I think they still do that today! I was at a race recently and saw a Top Fuel car puffing smoke out of a pipe, and as soon as he stepped on it and left, everything was fine!

I can take you down to my shop and show you all kinds of things we put on our cars that didn't do anything, just to get the other guys thinking too much. On *Swamp Rat XXVI*, you can look on the dash and there's a "traction dial." You can set it to "Less Traction," "Medium Traction," or "More Traction." The whole idea was I could set that dial to wherever I had to, depending on how good or how bad the track was.

At the 1971 NHRA Springnationals in Dallas, Texas, John Wiebe set low e.t. with a 6.47-second pass after I had already parked *Swamp Rat XIV* in the trailer. I pulled my dragster back out and on this run took low e.t. honors with a 6.44-second run.

Connie Kalitta himself was over there with his head inside my car, and I caught him trying to find out what that was connected to. It was connected to nothing!

In drag racing, you have to try to get whatever advantage you can over the other guy.

Then we built a rear-engined car for Tom McEwen. I think it was the first rear-engined chassis that came off the jig that wasn't for me. We put this bar underneath the seat and ran a valve spring between them. We put this adjuster on it so that you could tighten the spring or loosen the spring between that bar and the seat and told McEwen it was to adjust the traction … and he swore by it!

I actually did have something that was there for a reason, but I told everyone the opposite of what I used it for. I had an extra fuel jet coming off the main fuel line, and I had a valve on the dash that would activate it. I told everyone that on a run when I was nearing the finish line and the engine was getting hot and close to burning a piston, I'd open the valve and send more fuel into the motor to richen it up.

Actually, I was doing just the opposite! I'd get out to the top of low gear, hit that valve, and lean it out, and today, we know that's the best way to run the fuel system. But back then, I never saw anyone else use that kind of setup.

One year I was in the final round against Gary Beck in Rockingham, and I tried another trick. We were in the lanes before the race, standing around, when I took my little pillbox of fuel jets and start making some "adjustments."

He said, "What are you doing?"

I said, "Well, I'm just putting some bigger jets in to lean this thing out, because I want to really be hauling ass when I get down at the top end."

He was watching me, and he thought I was changing the jets, but I was really leaving it the way it was!

What did he do? He went straight back to his car and put in some bigger jets—and when we finally raced, he proceeded to burn his car to the ground!

THE WHEELS OF PROGRESS

By the mid-1960s, NHRA drag racing was well on its way to converting from the old flagman starter to the new electronic starting system, which we all know today as the Christmas Tree. Big Daddy remembers how he and his fellow racers received the new system.

We all hated the new system. By then, we had all gotten pretty good at reading the flag starter just by watching his eyes. We could read the muscles in his arms and how they tightened up just before he threw the flag up. The first Christmas Trees only had about three lights, and then they went to more lights before they came back to what they are now. At first, there were no staging beams or pre-stage beams; there was just a single beam across the track at the starting line. It didn't take us long to figure out that all you had to do was stay back from that beam a little way and you could leave pretty darn early on that thing!

We had a few things we did to keep them from bringing us up any closer, because they had officials who would push the cars up to the line by hand. We'd whack the throttle, and that would send them back real quick—wherever we happened to be would be fine with them. Outside the car, you can imagine how loud it was if you were right next to it.

We actually had it worked out that if you were far enough away from the beam, you could leave damn near on the first yellow! Then they designed the pre-stage and stage beams, and that pretty much put a stop to that.

I have a picture of the dragster with the tires smoking, and the Tree has only come down to the second yellow—and it doesn't go red!

The older drivers hated it when the Tree came in. We eventually adjusted to it, but we really didn't want it. There was a story of one guy in a roadster who just plain drove over it!

FIRE BURNOUTS

The whole idea of fire burnouts happened by accident. The first three drivers I ever saw who had their tires burst into flames—this was during the run when the tires were spinning and got hot and the heat

"TV" Tommy Ivo and I get ready to match race in 1973. Ivo is in the far lane executing a fire burnout, a tremendous crowd pleaser that I helped popularize.

from the exhaust combined to cause a fire—were Connie Kalitta, Bobby Langley, and "Flaming" Frank Pedregon. I mean, they were down the track and then they were flaming the tires. There may have been other drivers doing that, but those were the three I saw with my own eyes.

But fire burnouts were different. I was in Orlando one night, and we were doing our burnout with traction compound. Now the compound we were using—we called it *glue*—was very volatile. RFI made it, and it was a thinner version of the glue that used to come with those old tire patch kits. It softened the rubber, and it really worked great.

So I made my burnout, and because there wasn't a lot of room around the starting line at this track, this was all pretty close to the starting line. When they

Bob Taafe has just splashed traction compound in front of my slicks at a race in Union Grove in 1973. With a stab of the throttle, I perform a burnout.

backed me up, I rolled right back into the puddle of the traction compound. It was getting pretty stringy by then, and some of it got onto my exhaust pipes. The next thing you know, my two tires are on fire! Now, the guys on the crew jumped back and I gave it a little whap to get the tires to spin and get out of it. It was spectacular!

The fire burnout was born.

THE BEST AT THE BURN

Tom (T.C.) Lemons was the best at getting us set up for those fire burnouts. He knew just how much traction compound to pour in front of each tire and

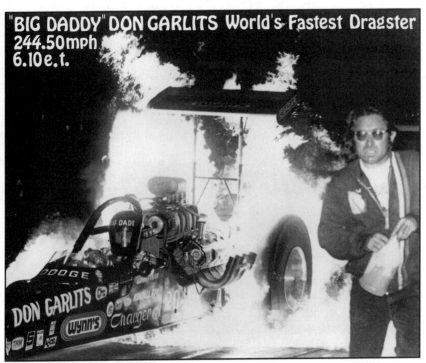

"BIG DADDY" DON GARLITS World's Fastest Dragster
244.50mph
6.10e.t.

One of the most memorable fire burnouts of my career is shown here. At Lakeland, Florida, in 1972 my dragster erupted in flames in the burnout box after T.C. Lemons, (foreground) poured traction compound under the tires. T.C. was considered one of the best when it came to "juicing" the track. I went on to beat the late Clayton Harris, who was driving Jack McKay's *New Dimensions* dragster.

what it took to get it strung out. I didn't spin it real hard to start with; I just gave it a little zing, and that would send some of the loose stuff right up on the exhaust. I'd look for just a little flame, and that told me I could really light 'em up!

The NHRA had cameras on us all of the time, and they tried everything they could to catch us lighting that compound with a match, because had they caught us doing that, we'd have been disqualified. But we never used a match to light anything, and we had some of the most spectacular fire burnouts the NHRA ever saw. And, of course, the crowd loved them.

THE FIRE'S OUT

Burnouts all came to a head at Indianapolis in 1969 at the U.S. Nationals. No matter how much traction compound there was out there all weekend, everyone had to put their own compound down when they ran. Now the burnout boxes were off to the side at Indy because they had to have a way for the stockers to get up there without going through the compound. When I got up there for my first run, there was so much traction compound in that box you could have floated the *Queen Mary* in it! Tommy came running over with our bottle of compound, but I gave him the high sign not to put any more down. I got into the box, and there was compound everywhere. I gave it that little spin just to get a little of it up on the headers, and suddenly, the box lit up! And to make it worse, at the same time there was another car in the other box and the two boxes were joined. So now you had both boxes and this other car on fire! Nobody got hurt, but it was one incredible fire!

It's a wonder that the guy who poured the compound over in the other lane didn't get hurt. He was over there pouring more in the box, and there were a couple of inches of it down already. I just rolled right up to the line and made my run, but the fire and smoke billowing everywhere were unreal.

Well, that was the end of traction compound in the NHRA. From then on, it was water only.

But the most spectacular fire burnout I ever saw was done by Flip Schofield in Marion, Ohio. It wasn't intentional. He had his crewman pour down the "juice" in the box like they always did. But in those days, a lot of the guys who worked on the crews were just people who happened to be at the track; they weren't specialists like you have today.

Anyway, this guy, Ernie I think his name was, poured the compound in front of one tire and then the other and went around to the front of the car to help Schofield roll into it. They weren't planning on doing a fire burnout, but it took this guy so long to pour the stuff and get around to the front that the tires had splashed some compound up on the headers. It all burst into flames.

Now this crew member dropped the bottle of compound, and as he tried to get out of the way, he tripped and fell right in front of the car. Schofield couldn't move out of there because he would have run this guy over! By the time they got this guy out of the way, Schofield hit the throttle to get out of there, but the tires were already burning and they both exploded right off the wheels. Finally, he was sitting there on his rims with fire all around him!

Somehow, he got out of there unhurt!

GARLITS VS. CARBONE ... IN EVERY ROUND!

At that same race in Marion, Ohio, Steve Carbone and I raced in five straight rounds. This was an AHRA event, and they had a special "break rule" that said the low elapsed time loser from the previous round would come back if anyone broke. I beat Carbone in the first round, and he had a real quick car. He had the low e.t from all of the first-round losers, and the guy I was supposed to race in the second round broke. So Carbone came back and I outran him again! It was incredible! The same thing happened in every round!

Let me tell you, those guys had it all worked out for the final round, because I was supposed to run Don "Mad Dog" Cook and he couldn't get anywhere near me. They knew Carbone was the only one who had a shot at beating me. When Cook made his burnout, he pulled it right over to the center of the starting line in front of the Christmas Tree and stopped. He said, "I made my burnout and it just shut off." But that was bullshit.

Carbone already had his engine running and pulled right up to the starting line!

So I had to race Carbone again, and I beat him again. The local newspaper ran a story that said, "It was a weird drag race, as Garlits beats Carbone five times in one day."

How embarrassing can it get, right?

"THE GREAT BURNDOWN" REVISITED

At the U.S. Nationals in 1971, Big Daddy faced Steve Carbone in a dramatic Top Fuel final round, in which each driver stubbornly waited for the other to stage. As history shows, Big Daddy finally bumped in first and was beaten by Carbone, three years after they had met in another Indy final with Big Daddy taking that victory. There was more to that 1971 confrontation, a race that has become an unforgettable tale within the legend and lore of the NHRA—"The Great Burndown."

I had been running in the 6.20s all weekend, and the rest of the field, for the most part, was running in the 6.50s. Carbone's best had been in the 6.60s. Everyone knew I just had too much for him.

Someone who had probably been sent over by Carbone's guys came by my pits before the finals, kind of stood back on his heels, and said, "Steve Carbone wants everyone to know that there's no way he's going to stage first when you two race!"

Well, I knew why he was saying that. The longer he took to stage his car, the longer it would take for him to be outrun! I'd have done the same thing! If he didn't stage, he still hasn't been beaten! And maybe if he waited long enough, I'd run out of fuel or blow up. Anything could happen!

I should have thought it through, but that idiotic German temper of mine got the best of me, and I was thinking, "My engine can run just as long as his can. My engine's got aluminum heads and will stay cool, but that 392 of his has iron heads and, in fact, was pinging and detonating all day long, so I have nothing to worry about!"

Well, finally I did stage first and got beat because my engine had those aluminum heads and stayed cool, but the longer I sat, the more power I made. I already was making all kinds of power. But in hindsight, what I should have done was make my burnout, pull right up to the line, and bang, stage my car. He would have said, "Wha' happened?" But I didn't always make the right decisions. I'm only human. I could have had nine U.S. Nationals championships instead of eight. But it was my own fault.

There really wasn't any rule that said either driver had to stage in a certain time. But if one driver staged, the starter would motion the other guy up to the line and, ya' know, he could take his time pulling up and go real slow. But if he stopped and didn't keep pulling up when the starter directed him to, the starter would signal the tower to activate the Tree and that it was going to be a single run. Then he'd look toward the driver who hadn't staged and do this *(Big Daddy makes a slashing motion across his throat with the side of his hand)* and he was all through.

Actually, I was always having some kind of run-in with Carbone. He was fierce. We raced a lot, and I honestly don't remember him beating me except that one time at Indy. I'm not saying he didn't ever beat me other times, but I don't recall it if he did. We raced a lot of match races, and I'm pretty sure I won them all. But he was a tough, tough competitor.

DEADLY COMPETITION

John Wiebe was another tough one. And I'll never forget what happened with him and Jeb Allen in Tulsa. Worst-looking accident I ever saw. They both shook and both got together. It was a wonder nobody was killed. But there were pieces of race car in every direction. Wiebe broke his leg, and that was about it.

But I was in the other lane, racing side by side with Marvin Schwartz in Tucson, when he hit the timing lights and was killed. I was in the tower at Indy in 1996 when Blaine Johnson hit the wall and got killed. And, of course, I was at Indy in 1969 when John Mulligan died in that horrible crash. There was a stud on the aluminum flywheel that somehow came around and sliced open the oil pan enough to get that nitro oil, which was under pressure, to shoot out on that red-hot clutch. The heat from that fire must have been incredible.

And I was the next one in line to run. I just shut the engine off. I didn't feel like racing any more that day.

Jimmy Nix had a huge fire at Pomona that was one of the biggest I'd ever seen. He got upside-down and backward with fire everywhere.

But I think the real danger to a driver is a hard impact. That was all that was going through my mind in Englishtown that time I went up and over backward. In my mind, the whole time, I was saying, "Please don't hit anything! Please don't hit anything!"

What I don't understand is why they don't have some kind of barrier between the lanes. Nothing too tall so you can still see the cars but something just high enough to keep a car from crossing over into the other lane and hitting the car over there. Think about that crash that Gary Scelzi had with John Smith in Brainerd a couple of years ago. If there had been some kind of barrier down the middle of the track, that bad collision between them never would have happened.

"IMPRESSING" KING HOGAN

 King's real name was Charles, and his son is Richard Hogan, whom a lot of people know as a pretty good tuner and who has worked with me a few times over the years. But it wasn't long after Grady Pickle told me that he didn't want to race King Hogan that I ran into him up at Zephyr Hills when I had my 1940 Ford with the Mercury engine. I was just a kid, and I had been keeping my eye on the "King," so on this particular day, I thought I'd impress him with my knowledge, right? I walked over to his 1934 Ford, and I said, "Ooohhh, I see you've got a 1942 distributor there on your flathead." It was pretty easy to tell, because that was the only year they had that kind of cap configuration, so I knew right away just by looking at it that it was from a 1942 Ford.

And he said, "That ain't nothin' like Ford ever made."

Well, what he had was a Harmon & Collins dual-coil ignition with the 1942 Ford distributor cap on it. I didn't even know a dual-coil ignition when I saw one! So much for impressing him with my knowledge!

"LOVE AT FIRST SIGHT"

Drag racing had a real bad reputation back then. It was all black leather jackets worn by a bunch of hoodlums in 1952. The NHRA was one year old and was struggling to give drag racing some respectability out in California, but a young lady just didn't bring a drag racer home to meet Daddy! It was about that time I met Patricia Bieger, who was out water-skiing with a friend one day at Lake Magdalene. We really hit it off right away. It was instantaneous, love at first sight.

I asked her for a date, and she accepted. When I pulled up to the front of Pat's house, her father looked out the window and saw my 1940 Ford with the cruiser skirts, Flipper hubcaps, and dual exhausts about to pick up his sweet young daughter, who was an honor student at Hillsborough High. I probably didn't make the best first impression.

But for me, like I said, it was love at first sight. It really was. I knew right from the beginning that this was the girl I wanted to marry. So the next day, I went out and traded my 1940 Ford for a bone stock 1950 Ford that I drove every day. At that time I was working at the American Can Company, and when I drove to work in that completely stock Ford, people were asking me, "What did you do with that 1940 Ford with the souped-up engine?" And I basically said, "I've gone legit!"

So for one year, I drove to bowling, roller-skating, and dancing in that 1950 Ford. But I was back into racing before long.

RETURN TO THE STRIP

About a month after Pat and I got married, we were out one Sunday heading to a recreation area that was very popular at the time called Bok Tower. You could have picnics there, and there were concerts and family events all of the time. We really enjoyed it. That afternoon, on the way out there, we drove by this little airfield that had been used during World War II and saw a sign hanging out front that said, "Drag Races Today." So I said to Pat, "Look, honey, there's a drag race today. Let's go in and just see what's going on."

When we got to the gate, the fellow at the entrance said, "Fifty cents each to get in. Do you want to run it?"

I said, "Sure, I might like to give it a try." And he said, "That'll be 50 cents more."

So we went in, and if I wanted to run my 1950 Ford, I'd run in the Stock class. The only thing I had to do was take off the hubcaps and the fender skirts. They didn't want anything like a loose hubcap flying into the spectator area and having it hurt somebody. You really couldn't call what they had a crowd because there weren't a lot of people there, and the ones who were there were parked right up at the edge of the runway where we ran.

Remember, drag racing was a brand new thing in those days and there wasn't a lot in the way of safety.

Well, by the end of the day, I had won my class. I was only running about 20-second elapsed times, but Pat was really excited when they gave me this little trophy that couldn't have cost more than 50 cents. This was really the beginning of the whole idea of awarding trophies for winning a drag race. I still have the trophy in my office at the museum.

King Hogan was there that day, and he was racing his 1927 Ford T-roadster I had first seen him driving back when I was out cruising with Grady Pickle. It had a V-12 Lincoln engine, and it was quick. He won Top Eliminator that day, and his trophy was much bigger than the trophy I had won. I knew right then that I wanted to beat King Hogan more than anything else.

BEATING THE KING

Pat and I went home to our little house that we had built in North Tampa and talked about what we were going to do to beat Hogan. We decided to buy a 1936 Ford and hot-rod it enough to beat King. Let me tell you, we worked and worked on that car day and night to make it a decent race car. I was working in a friend's body shop at the time. At the end of the day, I'd come home and Pat and I would work on the 1936 practically all night. Sometimes Pat would sleep on the seat

My 1940 Ford convertible pulls to the starting line at Zephyr Hills, Florida. Next in line with his fenderless 1934 Ford Coupe is King Hogan, the first driver I dreamed of beating.

of the 1950 Ford while I worked. I'd grab a shower, go back to work at the body shop, and start the whole process over again!

We put a 276 cubic-inch flathead in that 1936 with three carburetors and an Isky cam and had that car looking real swoopy. I really liked it. The fenders were removed, and the body was channeled six inches over the frame.

In a few weeks, we took the 1936 out to the races at Lake Wales, but we still couldn't beat Hogan. Another fellow I knew, Dick Schofield, had a used car lot, and he was planning on building a 1927 T, but instead, he sold the chassis and body to me. Pat and I took it home, and underneath a tree in our yard, I built the 1927 T. I had sold the 1936 to get enough money to put into the T, and when it was done, we went back to the drag races.

But this car still wasn't quick enough to beat Hogan. He was running in the low 13s, and I was in the high 13s. Close, but not close enough.

Now, I had noticed that his V-12 Lincoln didn't spin the tires when he launched. That V-12 made more power, but it also was heavier, and in this situation, the extra weight was a benefit. My car was spinning the tires, and after it hooked up, I could run with Hogan, but that advantage he had off the line was the difference. So I decided to lengthen the wheelbase on my car, figuring that would help eliminate the wheelspin.

It did.

The next time I raced Hogan, I beat him. That was a pretty exciting thing for Pat and me. It had been a few years since I had first seen King Hogan beating all comers back on Hillsborough Avenue, but now I had outrun him. I'll never forget it.

BIG DADDY
VS. THE NHRA

The first NHRA race I ever entered was in Lake City, Florida, not long after I had beaten King Hogan. I had been looking at the hot-rodding magazines from California, and guys were running dragsters out there. I decided I could make my 1927 T into a dragster.

I took off the body, moved the engine back, and mounted the seat behind the rear end. Now I had a dragster, and suddenly, I was outrunning all of the guys around Florida with it. The NHRA, which was still trying to put together a real national organization, had its Drag Safari program traveling all over the country, and the 14th event of the series was coming to Lake City, Florida. This series didn't have any points like we know it today. It was just a way for the NHRA to introduce the country to drag racing.

There were a lot of guys with some money in their pockets who could follow the series around, and because they were giving the NHRA so much support by attending so many of their events, they were a lot tighter with the NHRA people. I was some local guy from Tampa whom they had never heard of, so I didn't get the same kind of treatment.

Well, I had to work all day Friday heading into the race at Lake City, so I didn't show up there until Saturday morning. They took a look at my car, and they wouldn't pass it through inspection. Chic Cannon was running the technical inspections, and he told me my roll bar needed to be braced. That sounded fishy to me because Calvin Rice's dragster didn't even have a roll bar, and he was competing in NHRA races in California. His car had been featured in a lot of hot-rod magazines. Next, Chic told me the carburetors needed to have shields. There were all kinds of little things that had to be changed or added, so I had to go out to town and buy whatever I was going to need to get through inspection. By the time they finally waved me through, it was four o'clock on Saturday afternoon. I had time to make one time trial and then come back Sunday for eliminations.

On Sunday, I beat my friend George Breen in the final to win my dragster class. He had a pretty good car, one of the only ones there that actually had a sponsor, "Norton Brothers Garage." King Hogan was there and had replaced the V-12 Lincoln with a Cadillac V-8 engine, but he got beat in his Open Gas class eliminations by Joe Travis.

Joe Travis and I wound up meeting in the final for Top Eliminator, and it looked like it was going to be a good race, but he had a distributor rotor break during the run and his engine quit. I won it pretty easily. I was running in the low 12s at about 108 mph, and had Joe's car not broken, it was capable of running those numbers, too.

SNAPSHOT

Eric Rickman from *Hot Rod Magazine* was there, and he took pictures of me standing there with the trophy. I was really anxious to see my picture in the next issue of the magazine, but when it came out, there were no pictures of me winning at Lake City. Just a little item printed down at the bottom of the page. But quite a while after that, it could have been 10 years or so, they finally ran the picture. I can't imagine anything like that happening today.

CLUBBED

I belonged to the Strokers Car Club at the time, because belonging to a car club was what guys did back then. The Strokers had a party after the race in honor of Pat and me for winning the entire race. None of the other members of the club even won a class. They gave us a little tea set for winning, which was nice.

But then, the club president, Gene Tinker, announced, "Well, I guess you'll retire now."

I said, "Why would I do that?" and Gene said, "Because you're never going to beat the Californians."

I thought to myself, what does he see when he looks at me?

BIG DADDY
VS. THE NHRA II

In 1957, right after Emery Cook went 166 mph, the NHRA banned nitro because they thought it was too dangerous. Not everyone switched over to gasoline. I didn't, Cook, Setto Postoian, Bobby Langley, and a bunch of others didn't. We kept running fuel. We just went over to the AHRA, the ATAA, or the International Timing Association of America. There were three sanctioning bodies that kept Top Fuel alive, and it was an advantage to them when the NHRA banned fuel.

The NHRA was still mostly a little California organization that had a big race in Great Bend. They really hadn't established themselves nationally.

Now, those other racers I just mentioned kept racing in Top Fuel. When you grouped us all together, I was the leader of the pack. It came down to "Don Garlits kept Top Fuel alive." But I didn't know it at the time. I was just a guy out there racing. I was barnstorming all over the country at these little podunk drag strips, and I had gotten some notoriety by then. Mickey Thompson made the switch to gas. You never saw him running nitro at any of the events being held by the other organizations. He was a big supporter of the NHRA. Tommy Ivo stayed away from fuel. He kept running gas, set the record at 180 mph, and didn't switch back to nitro until the NHRA did. Eddie Hill ran gas that whole time, too.

The NHRA stayed with gasoline-only from 1957 through 1962. They ran fuel again at the 1963 Winternationals, and then they lifted the ban in 1964. It must have really put a thorn in their side, ending the ban, because the NHRA has never liked having to say, "Ya know, we made a mistake. Let's go back to the way that it was." When was the last time you heard them say that? Well, they had to do it in 1964.

They even bought the ATAA to try to stop them from running Top Fuel. They bought it and closed the whole series down. They just gave the owner the money

Here I am in between races in 1965.

and said, "Here, now there's no ATAA." But they never got to Jim Tice, the owner of the AHRA, and the International Timing Association never tried to get big, so they weren't that big a threat. But by 1963, Tice had gained some serious ground. Their big race at Green Valley was becoming prominent, he was soon putting together a series, and the AHRA was growing.

But the NHRA never forgot that I ran at the races where you could run nitro. The next big confrontation was in 1960. That year the NHRA teamed up with NASCAR, and they ran the first NHRA Winternationals at Spruce Creek, which was an old airfield near Daytona Beach, Florida.

This was a different kind of drag race. This was all about who had the highest top speed, and it was tied into Speed Week. We ran every day that week, and they had a Top Eliminator winner every day, who won a small trophy, but the big prize was for whomever ran the fastest top speed of the week. They got a gigantic trophy.

I had to work all week, so the earliest I could get down there was Friday. I showed up on Friday, and guys like Joe Jacono, a big NHRA runner, had been there all week. Louis Carden, another big supporter of the NHRA, had been there all week running his car before I showed up, and I hadn't really been driving all that much. Malone had been doing most of the driving, and suddenly, Don Garlits rolled in with a gas dragster.

I was there with my brother's gas car that had a blown Chrysler Hemi engine. I was even wearing Art

Malone's helmet. Believe it or not, who came over to help me unload the car but Wally Parks! He was smiling and happy while he gave me a hand getting the car off the trailer!

Now, I'd never run gas, and they figured I wasn't going to do shit! Well, I raced right through the field, and the next thing you know, it's Carden and me running in the final for Top Eliminator. I've already outrun all of the blown cars, and now I'm running Carden's car, which is a C/dragster, unblown.

Let me explain something here. That's the way they did it back then. If you were the winner in the dragster class, you then had to run the lower-class cars for Top Eliminator—not Top Fuel, or Funny Car—but Top Eliminator. Heck, they should do that now—then you'd only have one big winner! You'd see how fast John Force would get into Top Fuel after losing a few times. The dragsters will outrun the Funny Cars most of the time. But back in those days, it wasn't always a sure thing for the dragsters to win. They could break, spin the tires, or get out of shape. Roadsters would win Top Eliminator sometimes. The Henslee & Cook roadster won Top Eliminator all of the time out there in California.

Well, it was Carden in his little unblown Chevy-powered C-Gas dragster and me in the Top Eliminator final on Friday night. In those days, you had a flag starter, and sometimes he'd have a red flag along with the green flag. He'd look at one driver, and the driver would nod that he was ready. Then the starter would look at the other driver, and he'd nod that he was ready. Then the starter would wave the green flag to start them. But if out of the corner of his eye he saw one driver leave too soon, he'd wave the red flag and the cars would have to come back and start again. It was a "no start," and you'd turn around and line up again.

The rule was that there could be as many as three tries for a good start. On the third restart if anything happened, it didn't matter; it was a race. And I had seen the Californians pull that when I had raced them in Houston earlier on. They used every one of those starts. They'd get that jump, have to start again, and do it a second time until finally they raced on the third try. That's when I'd jump because I knew the third one was the last one.

Well, Carden knew he'd need to leave on me to beat me because he was in that smaller, C-Gas dragster. So he jumped on the first start, and the starter waved the red flag. I was trying to get a little edge on the start myself, but when I saw the red flag, I just circled back around across the track and drove back toward the starting line. There was no barrier, no fences, nothing in the way.

When I got back to the starting line, Carden's engine was shut off and he was just sitting there. The starter signaled to me to cut off my motor and that we'd have another start. Suddenly, Wally leaned down into my car and told me I'd been disqualified for crossing the centerline!

I said, "I crossed the centerline after the starter waved the red flag! There was no race going on when I crossed it!"

Wally said, "Oh no, we have a rule. You can't cross the centerline."

I said, "What kind of a rule is that? Nobody told me anything about that! This is how we do it! We cross the centerline, come back around, and line up for another start! Carden wasn't even supposed to shut his motor off!"

Wally insisted, "Well, we've made this rule." Then I heard Carden's motor start.

The announcer said over the PA, "Louis Carden is going to make a single run because Don Garlits has been disqualified."

I said, "Like hell he's going to make a single run!"

Malone was in the Cadillac push car right behind me, and you really didn't have to push those dragsters very far to get them started. I waved to Malone to push me and get me started. Art didn't know or care who this guy in the gabardine coat was, so he pushed me ahead.

Wally was yelling, "No!" He came over to the Cadillac to try to stop us. He reached over and grabbed that big chrome ornament that 1950 Cadillacs had to open the hood, lifted up his legs, and was now riding on the hood of the car while Malone was pushing me! Wally had no choice! It was either jump on or get run over!

The dragster started, and I headed to the line right away. Carden was already gone. He was under way while

I was 10 or 15 feet behind the line, so I just nailed the throttle and I was off. I blew past Carden like he was standing still, and the announcer said, "Garlits wins the final, but Carden is the official winner of the race." I didn't give a damn who was the official winner. I had just beat Carden and kicked his ass after he was way out in front of me. Meanwhile, Wally was still hanging off the hood of that Caddy!

The next night I came back, and this time, I was real careful about all that starting line business. I outran Hoyt Grimes in the final and I went over 160 mph, which gave me top speed of the week. That was for the big trophy. For years, I told people I won the first Winternationals because I believed I did! I won Top Eliminator two nights in a row, Saturday and Sunday, and had the fastest speed and the biggest trophy!

But they actually gave Louis Carden the small trophy because he had won the most Top Eliminators that week. He had won just about all week and had won on Friday when they disqualified me. It wound up pretty close between Joe Jacono and him. But they never made a big thing about Carden winning, and I really wasn't aware of what they did.

Some time after that, I got a letter with a Santa Monica, California, postmark that said, "We're a group of big drag racing historical fans, and we'd like to bring something to your attention. Louis Carden won the most Top Eliminators at the first, so-called, NHRA Winternationals, and you only had Top Speed."

But the wording of the letter made it obvious that it was right from Wally's desk. He was straightening me out.

Here's another little part of this story. They sent me a copy of the *National Dragster* that had the article about the race, and if you look at it, there's a picture of Carden with his little trophy, but there aren't any pictures of me with my big trophy. They didn't publish that. Now, on that Friday night when Carden beat me in that crazy final, they actually presented me with three trophies. I got one for winning my class, A-Dragster; I got one for running low elapsed time; and I got one for running the fastest speed. And I was so angry about what had happened in that final that I told them, "You can shove these trophies up your ass!" I smashed them on the ground. By the time the entire event was over, I had cooled down, and they took pictures of me with all of the trophies I had won on Friday, Saturday, and Sunday. All of them were there because the NHRA had picked up the ones I had thrown down and repaired them all!

The sad part of this whole story? They were all in my office back in 1966 when we had a tornado, and we lost every one of them. It also goes to show you how cool Wally is. He never gets mad—only even!

A SHORT TRUCE

Everything just sort of smoothed out after that, and the NHRA contacted me to tell me they were going to do some Top Fuel testing in 1963 at the Winternationals in Pomona. Believe it or not, I actually led their campaign to get the drivers who had stuck with gasoline to come out and run with nitro again. A lot of those drivers were really unhappy with the NHRA because it was bringing back fuel.

I submitted an entry sheet and told the other drivers that we should all support this event. I told them we needed the NHRA to support Top Fuel and we should all turn out.

Top Fuel wasn't going to be the featured class at this event, but it got all of the publicity. Of course, the fans were all standing up and cheering when the fuel cars ran, and it was quite a deal. In the final I beat Art Malone in my car with the wing over the engine, and I have to give Bruce Crower credit for it because it was his idea. He said, "We have got to have more traction because the cars are so light and we have so much power. This wing is free. We'll get some downforce without suffering a lot of drag."

He designed the whole wing assembly and had a friend of his build it for us down in Chula Vista, California. But after we got it on the car, I had a problem with the NHRA because of it.

The famous wing car running at the 1963 Winternationals. It was the first application of a wing in drag racing, and the NHRA was reluctant to allow it. When I said that someday all dragsters would have wings, I was told I was "nuts." I won the race, beating Art Malone in the final.

When I got to Pomona, Jack Hart of the NHRA tech crew took a look at that wing and asked, "What is this? I don't know if we can let you run with this."

I said, "Jack, when the smoke clears, every dragster in competition everywhere will have a wing on it some day. Trust me."

He said, "Garlits, you are so wrong. That's the most obnoxious-looking thing I've ever seen."

Well, I think they all have wings now.

THE WING IS THE THING

After that, we were allowed to run fuel when we were going for the speed record. I went out to the Connecticut Dragway with the wing car and set the record there, more than 190 mph, and I think that's the only Top Fuel record that was ever set there.

PIT POLITICS

In 1962, the NHRA must have had some clout with Dodge, because Frank Wylie called me and he said, "We want you to build a gas dragster with the wedge motor and race it at the U.S. Nationals. We don't want you to run the 392 because we don't make it any more. Build a wedge to run on gas and it will run fine."

Well, we did that and went to Indy. The car was the runner-up to Jack Chrisman. Let me tell you a story that nobody knows.

It was Monday afternoon, Labor Day, and it was time for the final between Chrisman in the Mickey Thompson Hemi-head Pontiac and me. They had only one set of those heads with them, and one was cracked. This was going to be a good race, because we were running really well and they couldn't afford to give up a

I stand beside my dragster at Indianapolis Raceway Park during the 1962 U.S. Nationals. The coveralls I was wearing were also my driving suit, which was all that was needed before firesuits became mandatory.

cylinder. Well, they fiddled around and fiddled around and didn't call us to the staging lanes, because here was this California guy about to race this East Coast guy. They did what they had to do.

First thing you know, it was getting a little late in the day and it was turning to dusk. The announcement was made, "It's too dark to run. We'll run the race tomorrow." So wouldn't you know, Mickey had a cylinder head flown in, and that final round wasn't called to the lanes until noontime, which gave them enough time to get the engine repaired. Chrisman beat me, but that was really unfair for me and for Chrysler. It was my race, but they made sure Chrisman had the time he needed to get his engine fixed.

I never would have gone to that race if Chrysler hadn't told me to go.

NOT MY LINE

In 1963, I wasn't entered in the U.S. Nationals, but I built a car for the team of Cassidy and Winward. The car was called *Brief Encounter*, and it was identical to *Swamp Rat IV*. We delivered the car to him in Indianapolis, but the first time it went down the track, it scared them. So I got in it and drove it for them.

Well, I got all of the way to the final round, and this was the first year that the NHRA had the Christmas Tree at Indy. They had that Canadian fellow who wore the

Indian costume lining the cars up at the starting line, and he was placing me in the final. I had a spot I pulled up to every time that gave me just the right amount of lead time so that I could leave on the last yellow. I was racing Booby Vodnick in the Hirata and Hobbs car, and I pulled up to my spot and stopped. The Indian wouldn't let me stay there. They had figured it out. They knew there was a certain place that I had to have to get a good leave. He kept motioning to me to pull forward. I didn't want to go, and until he gives the high sign that I'm where they want me to be, they're not going to start the race. So they pulled me up right to that elapsed time beam, and I left on the last yellow. Sure enough, I went red. Vodnick was the winner.

I was really pissed about that. We had really worked hard, and how I lost that race really stuck in my craw.

ACROSS THE POND

In 1964, I agreed to race at the British Drag Festival that traveled to England for the NHRA. We went basically for expenses, but we were excited about going to England because it was a pretty neat deal. And it was a great trip. Pat and I never had so much fun in our lives. We had first-class accommodations on the SS *United States*, and the trailers with the dragsters were parked right out on the deck. It was like a dream for us. I got to go because I won the U.S. Nationals that year. That final was quite a story.

After winning the U.S. Nationals in 1964, the NHRA asked me to race in the British Drag Festival in England. This run set a new British land speed record of 8.09 seconds at 197.00 mph.

I am in the near lane, racing Tommy Ivo at the British Drag Festival. Note the body panels on my dragster have been removed. There were high crosswinds.

LIGHTS OUT

We ran really well at Indy that year and got all the way to the final round to face Jack Williams. I really didn't want to give this race away with a red light. I was thinking about what had happened to me the year before, and there was no way I was going to give this race away with a red light.

It was the same situation as before with the starting line crew getting you staged and me not wanting to roll in too deep. After we got staged, I played it real safe. I didn't try to jump on the Tree at all. But I looked over when the Tree went green, and Williams was already gone! Here's what I think: I think they had disconnected the red lights. They did it because they thought I'd really try to get the jump, and they didn't want me to foul! They were doing it to help me win! They wanted me to go to England as part of that tour!

I turned my car loose, and we began to gain on Williams. At the finish line it was sooooooo close. You had to have the electronics to decide who had won.

Now, of course, these were the days before instant replays or any television at all at drag races, so we could never look at the finish later, but my win light came on and I was the winner. We ran more than 198 mph to beat him. Connie Kalitta went 200 mph at that race and was the first to go 200 at a national event. I had the national record at 201.34 mph that I had run in that

Indy-winning car at Great Meadows, New Jersey, on August 1 at one of the divisional events.

But to this day, whenever I happen to bump into Williams, the first words out of his mouth are, "I won that race." The funny thing was that by trying to help me, the NHRA almost cost me another U.S. Nationals. At least, that's what I believe happened.

BAD TIMING

In 1965, we got an offer from someone who wanted to buy *Swamp Rat VI.* This was the car that won the 1964 U.S. Nationals, won the Dragfest in England, and had set the national speed record. They paid us $7,500 for it, and that was a pretty good price back then. They sent us the check for it, and the deal was done. Or so I thought.

But I had one more match race to go to with it before I delivered it, and that was at Great Meadows, New Jersey. I was making a run up there and the cable for the parachute broke. The chute didn't come out, I flipped the car over on some railroad tracks, and it got tweaked.

I brought the car back and told the guys who were going to buy it that I'd either build them a new chassis or fix that one, and they said, "We want our money back."

I gave them their money back and took the chassis back to the shop and stored it up in the loft. But we still have that car; in fact, it's in the NHRA Motorsports Museum, and it's totally restored. We fixed it, and some of the little details on it all came together at once.

When Pat and I were moving from Seffner into our new place in Ocala, we were going through the closets and found two of the original British Dragfest decals in there, and we didn't even know we had them. It helped to make the car look perfect.

Now, I lost track of the Enderle injectors we had on the car when we were racing it, but one day we were opening some boxes we had moved here that had been stored up in the attic and, lo and behold, there was that set of Enderle injectors!

PRA

The whole idea of a separate racing organization actually began with "The Burndown" in 1971. After Steve Carbone beat me in that confrontation, which the NHRA said had 100,000 people sitting there watching—which I doubt, but that's what they said— Carbone got a check for $3,000. That was his payoff. Plus, there may have been another $3,000 in contingency money, but it was never that much because sometimes the companies don't pay or they say, "Well, the decal isn't in the right place" or what have you. It isn't like getting another nice, big check right on the spot.

At the following SE NHRA Division banquet in Atlanta in January, following Indy in September, Wally Parks was in attendance and gave a speech. Afterward, I took Wally aside. I said, "Wally, that deal in Indy was a joke. Carbone should have gotten $25,000 for winning that race, not $3,000!"

He said, "No, no…Carbone got $6,000 for winning the race."

I said, "He got $3,000 for winning, and he still hasn't gotten the other $3,000 from contingencies. I know that for a fact. It's still just dribbling in. I'm telling you that he should have gotten $25,000 for winning that race!"

Wally looked at me and said, "Garlits, we are light years away from something like that."

I said, "Really?"

So I wrote him a letter and said that the Top Fuel winner at Indy should get $25,000, the Funny Car winner should get $25,000, and the Pro Stock winner should get $25,000. No funny deals. That's not counting contingencies; the contingencies would be on top of that.

I said, "If you can't do that, I'll find somebody that will—and we'll have the race on Labor Day!"

He wrote back to me and said, "You'll never be able to do that."

So I talked to some of the Top Fuel drivers and some of the Funny Car drivers. They seemed to think that it was a good idea. They said, "We'll support you."

We went ahead and formed an organization, the PRA—Professional Racers Association—and everybody who joined paid $100 for one certificate of stock. I went to Jim Tice of the AHRA and said, "This is what we

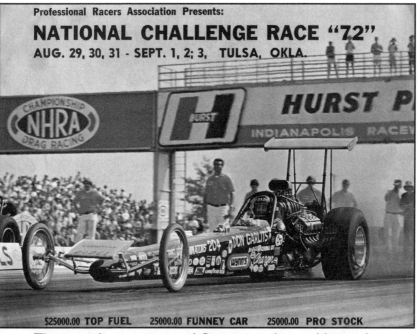

Professional Racers Association Presents:

NATIONAL CHALLENGE RACE "72"
AUG. 29, 30, 31 - SEPT. 1, 2; 3,   TULSA, OKLA.

$25000.00 **TOP FUEL**   25000.00 **FUNNEY CAR**   25000.00 **PRO STOCK**

This was the promotional flier created to publicize the PRA's first national event, which ran head-on with the NHRA's U.S. Nationals on Labor Day weekend in 1972. All of the professional classes received a winner's purse of $25,000, and the race is credited for changing the NHRA's prize money structure. Note the spelling miscue on "Funney Car."

want to do. Will you support us?" He said, "I think it's a hell of an idea and I'll support you; in fact, I'll put the money up!"

So we went to the bank and Jim withdrew $150,000 from his account. We took pictures of it in the vault and then deposited it in the PRA account. We had the money.

The race was going to be in Tulsa, Oklahoma, and we weren't going to pay a lot of round money. We were going to pay $500 if you qualified and $25,000 if you won. All of the drivers were fine with that. They understood that they got $500 for qualifying but no more money unless they won. They knew we were trying to make a point. And we did it. We had the race.

Tice and the rest of us thought about the risks involved with a venture of this size and what would happen if it rained on Labor Day. So we decided we'd have the race on Sunday and hold Monday in case we got rained out. That way, we'd be sure to get the race in. But that was a mistake.

That allowed Don Prudhomme, Tom McEwen, and Bill Jenkins to qualify at Indy on Thursday and not have to worry about getting bumped out because there wasn't hardly anybody there. Then, they could shoot over, race with us on Sunday, get back to Indy, and race there on Monday. And that saved the U.S. Nationals.

But it scared the NHRA.

The lowest contingency payout we had was $1,000. The least that our winners on Sunday walked away with was $37,500, and I think McEwen won the most, more than $38,000. Don Moody won Top Fuel.

The NHRA had to do something, so they went to all of the manufacturers and said, "You've got a put a stop to this. This could be the end of us." So the manufacturers went to Tice, who was pretty well connected with them, and told him he could still support the race, but that it had to be moved away from Labor Day. It would be better for everybody if he did that.

The manufacturers even put some pressure on me. "You don't want to kill the NHRA, do you?" they asked me. "They've done so much for the sport. They're the backbone of the sport. You don't want to do this, right?"

So we moved the race, and it just wasn't the same. We moved it to the week before Labor Day. Some guys came and some guys didn't, and, of course, it wasn't better for everybody because it allowed the NHRA to catch its breath. We had them on the mat, and had we stayed with it, the racers would have control of the sport today.

And by the way, the NHRA paid $18,000 to Gary Beck when he won Indy that year!

The NHRA said, "We were going to do that anyway. We were going to raise the purse, and it had nothing to do with the PRA."

I guess they weren't light years away from it after all.

MENDING THE FENCES

Wally Parks and I have mended the fences a little over the years, but not completely. If you look at that big book they came out with on their 50th anniversary, you can tell there's still a little resentment there. The publisher showed me the section about me that had originally been written for it. It was really nice, but it was taken out.

I think some of the newer people in management at the NHRA realize that was a mistake.

I've signed a bunch of those books and there's not a person who hasn't asked me, "Why did they do that?"

But our differences go back a long way.

RUBBER WAR

I headed out to Pomona in 1969 for the Winternationals with T.C. Lemons with a really good car, *Swamp Rat 12-B*. But there had been some talk about me doing some tire testing for Goodyear because the word was that they were going to make a big move into drag racing. I had always been an M&H guy, and when Marvin Rifchin of M&H heard the talk about me testing for Goodyear—I still hadn't tested for them yet—he got really upset.

A rare photograph of me making a burnout at Winternationals in Pomona in 1968 in *Swamp Rat 12-A*. I won six Winternationals titles during my career, more than any other driver.

Now M&H had this brand-new 10.85x16 tire that was different from the old, flat tires that, up to then, were designed to spin and smoke. This new tire was more of a balloon tire, and we were now headed for "smokeless." Rifchin only brought about 10 sets of them to Pomona, and when I got there, he didn't give me any of them. He told me, "All these tires are spoken for." I had always run M&H tires, but he must have known that once Goodyear got into the sport, their money would have overwhelmed him. He didn't like the fact I was going to be helping Goodyear come up with a good drag-racing tire.

Now, there were more new tires on their way to the track, and I could have gotten a set, but the plane bringing them to California was on the ground in Cleveland because of fog and couldn't take off.

PUBLICITY STUNT

Bob Russo, the NHRA's public relations director, came to me when I got to Pomona for the 1969 Winternationals. I was getting tech inspected—the day before we did any racing—and he said, "I'd really like to take you into Los Angeles all day Friday and do some promotion for the race for TV and radio."

I said, "Well, I can't give up Friday, Bob, I need to be here and get in line for qualifying."

See, in those days, you had to get into the staging lanes in the morning because they ran everybody according to how many cars were in the class. If there were 100 stockers and 15 dragsters, they'd run the stockers, and the dragsters would have to wait their turn. You had to line up at seven o'clock in the morning if you wanted to get a run in. If you did that, you'd probably get to run by 11.

We worked on the cars right in the lanes. It wasn't anything like it is today. Now, you work on the cars in the pits and they come and let you know when to start up there for your run. Today, you're guaranteed a chance at making your run. Then, you were guaranteed nothin'!

So I said to Russo that I needed to be there on Friday to make my runs. I couldn't possibly go with him.

He said, "If you were able to run any time you wanted to, how many days would you need to qualify?"

I said, "Hell, I'd need one afternoon! If I could run any time I wanted to, I could qualify on Saturday easily!"

He said, "I'll take care of it. You come with me on Friday, and I'll see to it that you can come right to the head of the line on Saturday and you won't have to wait at all. When you get up there, they'll stop everything and you can make your run on the spot."

I said, "That's a hell of a deal. I like that!"

So on Friday, I went all over Los Angeles with Russo doing TV and radio and whipping everyone up for the Winternationals. Back at the trailer, everyone was wondering what's going on because the car was sitting there, I wasn't around, and all T.C. was saying was that we were involved in some "secret shit."

On Saturday morning, the lanes were filled and all of the dragsters were lined up waiting to run. We were just lolly-gagging around the trailer, just taking our time fussing with the car, putting plugs in it, and massaging it here and there. Finally, we rolled it out and pushed it down to the staging lanes and moved right up to the front of the line.

The security person up there came over to us and says, "What the hell are you doin' here? Go to the back of the line!"

I said, "Nope, I run any time I want! Stop the race! We're ready to make a run!"

He said, "What are you talkin' about?"

I said, "Go get the event director! He'll set you straight! Go get him!" As I said this, I was putting on my firesuit and getting ready to make my run.

They brought Jack Hart over and he said, "What's goin' on here?"

I said, "I get to run any time I want to."

Hart looked me right in the eye and sneered, "Who says?"

I said, "Bob Russo says. You go get him."

He said, "Really. What did Bob Russo tell you?"

I said, "Bob told me I could run as many times as I wanted, when I wanted, and all I had to do was come up here to the front of the line. And I can do it because I spent all day Friday doing PR work for the NHRA."

I said, "Now stop the race. I'm ready to run."

They found Bob Russo, and they took him aside, away from me. They talked to him for a minute. Then he started walking over to me and he had a real hang-dog expression on his face.

He said, "Big Daddy, I'm so sorry. I didn't think it would be any trouble at all. I don't know what to tell you!"

Hart looked over and shouted, "Go to the back of the line!"

The story gets better.

We went to the back of the line, and eventually, we actually got to make a run. We ran on the old tires, and we went about 7.50 and needed a 7.48 to get in. In the meantime, the fog had lifted in Cleveland and the plane with the new tires was able to get to California.

We ran over to the M&H trailer and got a set of the new tires; we mounted them on the car and got back into the line to run. We actually got to the head of line in the very next group that was scheduled to go. An NHRA official walked over to the line of dragsters and shouted, "How many Top Fuel dragsters haven't made a run or have made only one run?" They went down the line and found all of the dragsters that hadn't made a run or had made only one run. Those cars were pulled out of line and moved over next to the fence in the staging lanes. There were about 10 cars in that line over by the fence, and I was the first one, all ready to go with my new 10.85 M&Hs.

They ran all of the stockers, and it finally was time to run Top Fuel.

Sonuvabitch…

They took the dragsters that hadn't been moved over near the fence and ran them!

I just went nutso!

So the NHRA said, "OK, OK, we're gonna let you run. A mistake has been made. We're gonna let you run."

So Freddie Dename and I were the first pair, and we got our engines fired up and were both ready to get our runs. Suddenly, word came down from race control, which was up in that little tower they had out there, "It's too dark to run. Shut them off!"

It was just dusk! There wasn't any problem with how much light we had! They shut us off, and I only got to make one run at the Winternationals. I missed the field with the only run I got to make. We would have gotten in like it was duck soup with a killer car like that. It was capable of winning the race.

Freddie came over to me and said, "Tonight, I'm gonna burn that tower down."

I said, "Please, Freddie, don't do that. It'll just make it harder on everybody. It won't solve the problem, and it'll just hurt all of the racers who came here from all over. Don't do it."

That night, I met Jack Hart at the hotel and we talked for a while, and I said, "Jack, this really wasn't right. Russo admitted he told me I could run whenever I wanted, and you should have made some kind of concession for me. People came here and wanted to see my car run on Sunday, and you could have done something."

He said, "We've got rules, and I have to obey them."

I said, "Why do you do things that always make people hate you? Wouldn't it be better if you did some things to make people like you?"

He said, "Everyone loves us."

I said, "No, they don't."

But it was too late to do anything about what happened. That was something I still have trouble forgiving them for.

SHIRLEY

Shirley Muldowney and I were at a match race in Union Grove one time, and we were pitted right across the aisle from her. Now, what a lot of people don't know is that Shirley's father had done quite a bit of boxing and was pretty good at it. He taught her how to punch by putting her weight behind her fist, and, let me tell you, she could hurt you. A woman wouldn't stand a chance against her, and she could hold her own against a lot of men.

So on this particular evening at Union Grove, I looked over at her pit. There was this fellow standing at her ropes, and Shirley was standing a few feet away from him near her car. He said something to her, and she sort of leaned in toward him as if she didn't quite hear him when he said it. Suddenly, as he was leaning in over the ropes, she hit him with an uppercut square on the jaw that sent his feet up in the air and his head down backward. He landed on the ground, knocked out colder than a mackerel!

She just turned around, walked back into her trailer, and never looked back. Later on, I went over there and asked her husband, Rahn Tobler, "What was that all about?"

He said, "Well, that guy made a remark to Shirley and she didn't like it."

I asked, "What did he say?"

Rahn said the man had made a revolting comment referring to Shirley's driver's seat. When she asked, "What did you say?" and he repeated it, she knocked him out.

THEN THERE WAS THE TIME AT MARTIN, MICHIGAN ...

I don't remember what year it was, I think 1975, but the promoter for this race up at Martin, Michigan, John Grivens, would always get a limo for us when we came to run up there. He'd take us to all of the TV stations and newspapers to promote the race. On this day, Shirley Muldowney and I were being driven around in the limo to Kalamazoo and Battle Creek to talk to the press. I hardly got a word in edgewise with the press because Shirley was telling them she had done this and she was going to do that. She kept going on and on about it, just PR. She was the center of attention because she was somewhat of a novelty as a woman in Top Fuel, and there had never been a woman in Top Fuel before, so I didn't get to say much about my deal. I couldn't say a thing about my records and all of my wins because they were all listening to her. I finally had enough of it.

Grivens wanted us to do it again the next day in Grand Rapids, so that night I called him and said, "John, just give me the list of the places you want me to go tomorrow and I'll go myself so I have a chance to talk to these people and it's not all Shirley's story."

He said, "Well, I don't really care what they write in the newspapers as long as we get lots of publicity. I'll tell you what, you probably have some things you want to do to your car, so don't worry about it. I'll pick Shirley up tomorrow and head up to Grand Rapids and take care of everything."

I said, "Well, John, do me a favor. Don't say anything to Shirley about this. I don't want to ruffle her feathers if I don't have to."

He said, "Don't worry about that. I won't say anything to her about it."

Well, Grivens was a real promoter, and he wanted to use this whole thing to sell a few more tickets.

The next morning, Shirley asked him, "Where's Garlits?"

"Oh, he's not coming today," he said. "He said he couldn't deal with being around you again all day. He's had enough of your act."

All day, Ron Barrow and I were working on the car in the motel parking lot, and we took everything apart so we could check all of it out. We suddenly heard this noise and looked up, and here came Shirley in her Lincoln—and she was coming fast! She jammed on the brakes right where we were, jumped out of the car, and came right over to me. She was not happy.

"I heard what you told Grivens about me, and I just want you to know that when I talk to Connie, I'm going to have him kick your ass!"

Now, let me tell you something. They don't make men much tougher than Connie Kalitta. He wasn't someone you'd want to mess with even on his best days, times when he wasn't his rough-and-tumble self. And if he wanted to come over there and kick my ass, there wasn't a whole lot I was gonna be able to do to stop him.

Shirley stormed back into her car and sped away, kicking gravel all over the place. Barrow looked at me and said, "What are you going to do?"

I said, "What can I do? We gotta go out there and race."

He said, "What about Kalitta?"

I said, "There's not much I can do about that. He's a killer. I hope he has some mercy on me because we go back so far, but I don't know what kind of power she has over him."

Later on, Kalitta got to the track from the airport, and they were pitted a pretty fair distance away from me. I could see them, but they weren't within shouting distance. Ron and I worked on the car through the late afternoon, but we still had some time before there was any racing. I said to Ron, "I can't take this any more. I'm going over there and talk to Connie. I can't be looking over my shoulder all night."

I walked over there, and I was just on the other side of the little road that he was pitted on and he saw me. "Hey, Garlits!" he yelled. "Come on over here! Shirley has something she wants to tell you."

I was in their pit now, and Connie called out, "Hey, Shirley, get your ass out here! Garlits is here!"

Shirley came out of the trailer, looked at me, and said, "Big Daddy, I'm so sorry for what happened this afternoon. I want to apologize, and I promise it'll never happen again."

I said, "That's OK, Shirley, I understand."

Connie did remember that he and I went back a long way. I used to stay over at his house when I was racing up in Michigan, and he used to stay at our house when he was racing down in Florida. We were pretty tight. And I was never more grateful for it.

MORE FUN WITH MULDOWNEY

I was down in Laplace, Louisiana, for a match race against Shirley Muldowney. The way we always determined lane choice was by one of us choosing it for the first race. I usually would just let Shirley pick her lane. And I had a working agreement with Rahn Tobler, her husband, that for the last race, whoever had low e.t. from the first two runs would get to choose. We never flipped a coin for lane choice in the final; we'd let low e.t. decide it. It was actually a system I used whenever I match-raced. On the first run, I'd have my softest tune-up in the car, let my opponent choose their lane, and use that first race to get a feel for the track. I'd use that first run to adjust my tune-up for the second run and hopefully run low e.t. to get lane choice for the final run.

Laplace always had a good lane and a bad lane. So Shirley's team picked the good lane for that first run because they had their car set on "kill." As expected, they beat me. I had run pretty good, and the run helped me figure out what I had to do. In our next run, I got the good lane and I beat her. I also set low e.t.

Now, I had already agreed with Rahn that whoever ran low e.t. would get lane choice in the third run. So when it was time to run, I pulled the car up into the lanes and stopped in front of the good lane. I was putting my firesuit on, and Rahn walked over to me and said, "We've got to flip for lane choice." I said, "We agreed that whoever has low e.t. gets to choose the lane this time."

"Yeah, but you ran low e.t. in that good lane and there's no way we can win in that other lane, so we've got to flip for it."

I said, "That's not what we agreed to."

Rahn said, "That's going to be a problem." He walked back over to Shirley's car. She was already sitting in it.

I got into my dragster, and Herb Parks, who was working with me, said, "What are we gonna do?"

I said, "Start it."

Remember, this was a match race. If you don't run, you don't get paid. There's not going to be some official who disqualifies you. You've got to make your runs.

After we started, Shirley started and we both moved up to the line, we staged, and I won the race.

When we turned off at the other end, Shirley stopped, got out of the car, and just stood there waiting. She didn't say anything to me. A few minutes passed, and Herb pulled up in our tow vehicle. Shirley walked right over to him and started giving him a good going-over about starting the car. And, of course, Herb was returning her fire, cussing and spitting profanities.

Shirley's crew arrived, and her son, John, went into the toolbox and got a big breaker bar. As he came up behind Herb, I yelled, "Herb, look out!" Herb turned around, just reached out and took that breaker bar right away from him. And John just started back-pedaling, bicycling we used to call it, and that was the end of it.

GARLITS AND GWYNN

Back in Dallas in 1986 we had something a little like that happen with Darrell Gwynn. Gwynn had been running well all day long—better than me, in fact. Even during qualifying he was getting there first, and I have to say he was always a good driver. On Sunday, he and I won in the semifinals and we were gonna race in the final.

It rained between the semis and the final, so we had a pretty long delay before they could dry the track and get ready to race. By then, it was dark, but we both got up there to the lanes and got the signal to fire. I never liked to start first, because sometimes someone would take advantage of that. I always waited to hear the other engine fire, and then we'd light ours right up. Well, they weren't firing. We waited and waited, and they didn't light.

Herb Parks looked over there and said, "I think they're having a problem. What do you want to do?" I said, "Start the son of a bitch right now!" Herb pressed the starter button, and we fired it up. I made my burnout, but by then, Gwynn still hadn't even started yet! Finally, they got it started. I had already done my burnout, and I was back to the ready line.

I was all through with my routine, and I pulled up to the starting line. Darrell had hardly any heat in his engine. I heard him chirp the tires a little before he staged, but when the Tree went green, I was gone and I beat him easily.

For years, they blamed Herb for starting the car when he did, but I was the one who gave the order to start. I saw Darrell not long ago at his book signing when his biography came out, and I told him, "Look, Darrell, drag racing is a lot more than a fast car that goes from Point A to Point B. It was then, and it still is today. The preparation in the pit is even more important than the ability of the car to get down the track. If your car isn't prepared in the pits and you can't start or you have some kind of trouble, you're a loser.

"That night, you couldn't start your car, it wasn't prepared right, and you had a problem. You were a loser. Just because you had a fast car, it didn't necessarily mean you were a winner."

He didn't like that too much. But the Gwynns were always good racers and good sportsmen. They didn't fool around up there, and they raced on the up and up. But Darrell always set his sights on me. I was the one he always wanted to beat. I called him "The Wolf."

THE COMPUTER

The Gwynns really were the ones who got me to put a computer on my car. I was always against computers. I wanted human beings to decide how to tune the car, not some machine. But around 1985 or 1986, they put a computer on their car, and Darrell's mother, Joan, was talking to Pat, my wife, and said, "We can't believe how much information we get from that computer."

So I broke down and put a computer on my car. And it's phenomenal what you can learn from it.

I think that's why Ray Alley may have been a little cool to me when I came back to the NHRA. He was involved in the whole development of the Race-Pak system, and for years, I was campaigning against the computers and telling everyone, "Don't get a computer. Let's be like NASCAR and keep computers off the cars."

I think that was another call I missed on.

My facial expression says it all. I am standing next to two fans while contemplating engine problems in 1976. I hated to lose, and I especially hated to lose due to mechanical trouble.

WHEN INGENUITY AND LUCK SHAKE HANDS

T.C. Lemons and I were up running at a race in Oregon back in 1969, and we were in the pits when this fellow came over to us holding a Donovan shaft. It was that big main drive shaft that fits into the clutch can, engages the clutch disks, and has that big female coupler on the back. This guy said, "Big Daddy, do you want this? I sold my car and I don't need it any more."

Now these shafts are all made to a certain size. There weren't very many of them that were totally alike. When you called Donovan to have one made, you told him what the dimensions had to be and they'd cut it to those figures; then they'd heat-treat it and send it to you. The car we were running at the time was really light, and we had reduced the weight just by trimming some things on the car, including the shaft like the one this fellow had given us.

Now Goodyear wanted us to have a set of their new tires for the race we were heading to at Sears Point. Terry Arfons and Mike Hopkins hand-delivered those tires to us all mounted on wheels, balanced, and ready to bolt onto the car. And they were really good tires and very big I might add.

When we got to Sears Point, I got out there for my run, and my main drive shaft broke! We needed another one, and remember, the odds of that shaft that had been given to us fitting in our engine were a million to one, but lo and behold, it fit! The only problem was that the shaft that snapped had a bearing pressed onto it and we needed to get that bearing off to put on the new shaft. We didn't have a press with us, so we took the broken shaft over to a chain-link fence, took the cap off one of the fence posts, and used that opening to drive the shaft down to get the bearing off. Of course, the shaft would go right down to the bottom of the inside of the fencepost, and it would stay there forever.

Everyone had some fun with us while we were hitting that shaft down through the bearing. They all yelled, "Hit it! Hit it! Hit it!" Finally, it came off and we got the new one on.

Here's the payoff to this story. We wound up winning the race by beating Dick Kalivoda in the final and running Sears Point's first six-second pass, a 6.99.

LIONS, 1970

O*n March 8, 1970, Big Daddy was competing at the AHRA Grand American Championships at Lions Dragstrip in Long Beach, California, when the clutch in his dragster exploded, scattering metal shrapnel in all directions, breaking his left leg in several places, and severing part of his right foot. It was this near-tragedy that inspired him to perfect the rear-engined dragster. There was another lesser known repercussion from that frightening accident.*

One of the most famous dragsters I ever built—which never ran. This front-engined car was built because early attempts at building a rear-engined car had been beset with problems. But rear-engined cars eventually succeeded, and this car was retired before it raced.

Very few people know about the young fan in the stands who had his arm cut off by the flying shrapnel. Now, when they put me in the ambulance, the part of my foot that was cut off was really still attached. It was just dangling. The ambulance was one of those old streamlined models that looked a little like a hearse. Everybody was so upset and so nervous about my accident that they carelessly shut the door of the ambulance while my severed foot was still sticking out! It chopped that piece of my foot off, and it fell on the ground!

Here's a rare shot of me testing the new rear-engined car at Orlando Speedway in 1970.

Somebody picked it up, wrapped it in a towel, and threw it into the ambulance with me, so it, too, went to the hospital. Well, Mickey Thompson knew this really skilled surgeon, Dr. Larson, who lived over in Burbank. Mickey got on the phone to him, and they helicoptered Dr. Larson to the hospital. He was actually there within five minutes after I arrived. But in all of the confusion, nobody had noticed what had happened to the kid in the grandstands. Plus, I had been racing Richard Tharp when I blew up. He had a red-light, but my explosion sent shrapnel through the electronic equipment and shut down the beams, so the red-light didn't stay on, which gave him the win.

Then, he had a huge explosion of his own at the other end and was seriously burned, but the one ambulance that was there was taking care of me. Nobody went down to take care of Tharp! He actually had to walk back to the starting line by himself!

Now, over in the grandstands there was all this commotion because a piece from my car hit this young teenage boy, Tim Ditt, and his arm was just about cut off. It was just hanging by some skin. When they got him loaded into the ambulance and brought into the hospital, they wheeled him in right beside me. Well, Dr. Larson took a look at this kid and said, "Oh, my God!" The doctor was holding what was left of my foot in this little plastic container, and he said to me, "Don, all I can do with this is use the skin to close your wound. I can't sew it back on. I'll give you a shot and knock you out, and in a couple of hours I'll have it all finished and you'll be fine. But if I take care of this kid now, I think I can save his arm. I'm here for you. What do you want me to do?"

That was a no-brainer. Dr. Larson took the boy into the operating room and saved his arm. And a year later, the kid was helping us in the pits and his arm was working just fine. It was miraculous. That Dr. Larson was really good.

The operation on the kid cost $16,000, and when he was lying on the gurney after they brought him in

from the ambulance, he was holding his pit pass and saying, "I got insurance! I got insurance!" Well, that's not
insurance, believe me. I asked the AHRA and Lions to
pay the $16,000 for the operation, but they wouldn't do
it. Eventually, the kid got a $50,000 settlement that paid
for the surgery and gave him a little money. That was all.

MORE FROM THE HOSPITAL

After my foot was sewed up after the explosion in
1970, I had been in the hospital three or four days
when I was sent to therapy. They had to teach me to
walk with a crutch. They wheeled me down to the therapy room, to these parallel bars, and when I got there, a
nurse, kinda like Nurse Ratched from the movie *One
Flew Over the Cuckoo's Nest*, said to me, "I want you to
stand up and put all your weight on your other foot
while holding yourself up on those bars."

I got up and put my weight on my left foot, and it
gave me the most excruciating pain I had ever felt in my
life! I let out a scream and told her it really hurt.

And she said, "Oh, c'mon, give it a try!" I tried it
again, and the pain was intense. I couldn't stand it.

She said, "Mr. Garlits, stop being such a big baby. I
thought you drag racers were tough." I said,
"Something's wrong here! You get my doctor down
here!" So I sat down in a chair, and they called my doctor down. I told him I had this terrible pain in my other

leg and couldn't put any weight on it. He said, "OK, we'll send you up to X-ray and maybe we can see what it is."

They took an X-ray, and when they looked at it, they saw my leg and foot were broken in five places! They were so preoccupied with the foot that got cut off, they never knew that my other leg had been hurt so badly!

I was really incapacitated. One foot was cut off, and the other was in this big cast. I was gonna be down for a while!

INDY, 1984

From the end of 1982 all through 1983 and into 1984, we were really busy with the museum, moving everything from Seffner up to Ocala. We literally made 100 trips back and forth to get everything up there. We hadn't built any new cars for a while; we had done a little AHRA racing and a few match races, but it had been pretty quiet during that time.

In the summer of 1984, Art Malone came up to Ocala to visit me. He checked out the museum, took a look around here, and suddenly said to me, "Let's go to Indy!"

I said, "Art, that's a hell of an idea. Let's get some tickets and go up there, because I need a break."

He said, "No, no, no, I want to go to Indy and race! Let's get a car and race!"

I said, "I don't have a car we can race."

He said, "Sure you do. What about that black car out there, *Swamp Rat XXVI?* We can race that."

I told him, "We can't race that car. It's outdated. It needs all kinds of stuff to be able to race now."

Art said, "I'll buy all of the stuff. I'll buy us the engines, the heads, the blowers, the clutch, and let's go up to Indy and race."

Well, including an L&T clutch, which is one thing we really needed, he spent about $20,000 for everything. Can you imagine getting all those things for only $20,000 today? And no computer. This was going to be tuning by the seat of your pants. That's how everybody was doing it.

We got Richard Hogan to join us, and Herb Parks came out to help us after Malone put all the money up. We got out to Indy, and the first thing that happened was that they parked us down in the pit area where there was always water when it rains. Sure enough, it rained, and we had water in our pits that was ankle deep.

Then we went out and set top speed of the event. It was obvious we were going to be a problem.

John Mullen of Diamond P, the TV production crew, came down to interview me, and they had to shoot the interview from a low angle looking up. They couldn't show the driver who had just set top speed of the meet standing in all of that water!

Well, we qualified somewhere in the middle of the field, and on Monday, we started mowing everyone

Declaration

WHEREAS, Donald "Big Daddy" Garlits, has brought national and international attention to the sport of drag racing by setting numerous speed records and winning more national races than anyone in drag racing history; and

WHEREAS, Don Garlits is universally acknowledged as the "King of Drag Racing", amassing a career high of fifty straight match races; and

WHEREAS, Don Garlits' experimentation and technical knowledge have produced a safer rear engine design for dragsters; and

WHEREAS, Don Garlits desires to establish a non-profit International Drag Racing Hall of Fame to honor and recognize those who have made significant contributions to the sport of drag racing and to encourage research to increase the safety of this sport; and

WHEREAS, the National, American and International Hot Rod Associations have wholeheartedly endorsed the concept of and the location for an International Drag Racing Hall of Fame;

NOW, THEREFORE, BE IT RECOGNIZED, that I, George Firestone, Secretary of State of the State of Florida, do hereby declare my support for an International Drag Racing Hall of Fame, to be located in Marion County, Florida.

IN TESTIMONY WHEREOF, I, George Firestone, Secretary of State of the State of Florida, have hereunto subscribed my name and have caused the official seal of the said state of Florida to be hereunto affixed in the city of Tallahassee, Florida, on this 31st day of May A.D. 1984.

George Firestone
Secretary of State

From the 14th Annual Induction for the Drag Racing Hall of Fame.

down. We had these little Avon tires on the bike wheels up front, because that was the way it was done then. The problem was that we were running more than 260 mph on every run, and they weren't designed for those speeds. On some of my runs, I was on the rims going through the lights! For the final round against Connie Kalitta, I borrowed the front wheels off Chris Karamesines's car! I had gold wheels on the front for that final!

Well, I beat Kalitta and won the race.

NOT THE END
OF THE ROAD

After I beat Connie Kalitta at Indy in 1984, Art Malone said, "Son of a gun, let's go to the Finals!"

I said, "Art, we've used up a lot of stuff to win this race. I don't think we have enough left over."

He said, "I'll give you another $20,000! Get whatever you need!"

And so we bought what we needed and we went out to the Finals in Pomona and won that, too! We beat Gary Beck in the final, and he had won the world championship the year before.

So Malone says, "There's no sense in you staying retired. Let's find a sponsor and come back next year."

We were able to pick up about $125,000 for the 1985 season and went back to the shop to build a new car, *Swamp Rat XXIX*. *Swamp Rat XXVII* was the turbine car, and *Swamp Rat XXVIII* was the sidewinder, so the car we built for 1985 was *Swamp Rat XXIX*, and it was a nice piece.

TURNED ON ITS HEAD

The week before the first race in Pomona in 1985, we had a match race against Gary Beck in Phoenix. Our car was running 5.40s, which is really quick. A 5.50 was considered a real good run at that time, so we weren't surprised when we beat Beck in the first two races without a problem. Then on the last run, the wing collapsed. I had built the struts out of lightweight streamline tubing, and at more than 260 mph, they just buckled.

I lost control, and it flipped over past the end of the track in the desert. I was upside down, and I really had my bell rung. I got out of the car, and I was filthy from all of the mud I slid into. There was mud all up inside my helmet, and I was a mess, so they cleaned me off and started taking me to the ambulance. But I wasn't thinking too straight at that moment.

I looked up, and I saw this truck drive up. This great big guy jumped out of the driver's side. It was Herb Parks, but I didn't know who it was. A woman jumped out of the other side, and I could tell it was my wife, but she looked like an older woman. I said to myself, "What the hell is going on here?"

They put me inside the ambulance, and by then, they've got the race car back right-side-up. When I looked at it out the window, it was the first time I had seen it since the wreck. I couldn't believe it. The seat was ahead of the engine! And on the side of the car it said "Garlits and Malone," and I hadn't been associated with Art Malone since 1959! Then I saw "In-N-Out Burger" and I thought, "What is that? Have I been cast into the future?"

Pat was in the ambulance with me, and I asked her, "Where am I, honey?"

She said, "You're at Firebird International Raceway."

"Where's that? What am I doing here?"

She said, "You just raced Gary Beck."

I said, "Who the hell is Gary Beck?"

"He's coming over. That's him."

"You mean that clown in the red firesuit?" My mind had been thrown so far back, I thought I'd never seen a red firesuit before.

I said, "I don't feel so good."

The attendant in the ambulance said, "This usually happens when someone takes a hit in the head. We'll give him a little oxygen, and that should clear up the fog. He'll be all right in a minute."

It was the weirdest feeling. I didn't know anybody, and I didn't know where I was. They gave me some oxygen, and by the time we got to the hospital, I knew I lived in Ocala, I remembered my Social Security number, and everything started coming back to me.

They released me from the hospital that night, and I went back to the track to get my trophy because I had won. The whites of my eyes were all red from how hard I had hit, but I got my trophy, went back to the hotel, and went right to sleep.

HOME AWAY FROM HOME

The morning after the wreck in Phoenix, I woke up and looked down into the parking lot. Herb and my nephews, Eddie Garlits and Billy Garlits, had the car all apart. Herb Parks told me he thought we could fix the car, but we'd need a place to do it. Well, Johnny West, the well known racer, lived in Phoenix and had a shop, so we called him up. His mother answered the phone and said Johnny was out of town for two or three days racing, but she didn't think it would be a problem for us to use his shop. She had a key, and we were welcome to come over and use whatever we wanted. She had no idea how much work we were going to do or how intense we were.

We took the car over there, and his mother gave me the key. We opened up that shop, got the car in there, and started working on it. His shop was just like mine. It had a mill, a lathe, and a heli-arc welder. We were ordering tubing, and we were coming along just fine. Three or four days later, Johnny came home and found us in the shop! You wouldn't have believed the look on his face!

At first, he got after his mom for letting us get in there, but after he calmed down, he jumped right in and helped out on the program just like one of the crew. And somehow, we got that car fixed.

POMONA, HERE WE COME

We made it out to Pomona for the Winternationals. Up in the grandstands was the owner of Super Shops, Harry Eberling, and Joe Hrudka from Mr. Gasket. Now, the *Los Angeles Times* had run pictures of the wreck in Phoenix and pictures of us

I smoke 'em at the 1966 Winternationals in Pomona. I won my first Winternationals title when it was held in Daytona in 1960.

repairing the car with a caption that read "Garlits Fixes Car for Pomona," so everybody had seen that. We raced the car all the way to the semifinals, and Harry said to Joe, "It looks like the old man wants to race! What do you say we get behind him?"

Harry and Joe cut a deal, and with all of our associate sponsors and the money they gave us, we got almost a million dollars to race. And that year, we won the championship.

LOST TREASURE

The week after Pomona, we had a match race up in Fremont against Shirley Muldowney. So we went up there, and we won the race in two straight rounds. One of the track officials hand-delivered my pay to my pit, but the only problem was, it was short $4,000. So I went down to the office to get the rest of my money, and I was told that my payoff was being cut because I didn't make three runs. They were deducting $4,000 from my winnings!

Well, that got me slightly worked up, and I told the promoter, "Look, I came up here with a car that I crashed in Phoenix; it's not handling that well, the roll cage is pushed over about six inches and the chassis needs to be back-halved. I ran low e.t. and top speed, won the race, and I could have told you when you wanted to book me that my car wasn't right and I wasn't coming. Now, I want my money!"

He was sitting at his desk, and he reached into the drawer and pulled out $4,000 cash. He was all ready because he knew I was coming!

I took the $4,000 and stuck it into my jacket pocket.

Five years later, I was in my closet cleaning out some of my old jackets, and I came across the one I had been wearing that day in Fremont. The $4,000 was still in the pocket!

I had deposited the portion of the prize money I got paid with a check, but I was so strung out and so upset about what had happened, and with all of the distractions of getting the sponsor, running the car, getting it straightened out, racing for the championship, and everything else that was happening, I forgot the money was in there. At the time I was getting ready to do something with those jackets, like give them away or put them on display or put them into storage. Is that funny or what?

THE RACE
TO END ALL RACES

In 1965, we were running pretty well. The year before, we won the U.S. Nationals, went to England with the British Drag Team and set a world record, and then in 1965 we came to Pomona still running the 392 and set another new record, more than 206 mph. We were on a roll.

But Don "The Snake" Prudhomme, was coming on the scene. He was the new guy, and he had that "Torque Master" car, which was a pretty fast car. We already had a few serious confrontations between us, so the old *Drag Racer Magazine*—no relation to any of the magazines we have today—decided they were going to have the race to end all races. This was going to be like a world championship fight between Prudhomme and the "Swamp Rat."

They put up this giant trophy, a lot of money, and put the race up for bids. Half Moon Bay in California got the event. The promoters told me, "This is it. You've got to come. We're going to decide who's the best."

I prepared a whole new car. I took *Swamp Rat VIII* and stretched the wheelbase out to 175 inches, and I called it *Swamp Rat X* because *Swamp Rat IX* was the Dart Funny Car.

We headed for California, and I had Connie Swingle with me. We made a quick stop on the way out for a match race in San Antonio, and we won that. When we got to California, we pulled into Bruce Crower's place, and Byron Blair mounted a real nice body on the car for us. Now, there was no time to do much because we had to leave for the race. We didn't have time for any fancy paint job, so we took a black spray bomb and painted the body. There was an alcoholic sign painter down the street, and he came up and just brushed my name on the car with silver paint. Well, we got up to Half Moon Bay and I won the race, but there are a couple of funny things about what happened. They were so sure that Snake was going to win the race that they already had his name engraved on the winner's trophy and my name on the runner-up trophy! Instead they had to take the plate from the runner-up trophy and put it on the winner's trophy. But they couldn't even do that, because that plate wasn't made for it, so they just laid it on the big trophy!

And I think the trophy girl was hoping Snake would win, because when they took my picture after the race, she didn't look very happy about having to be in the picture with me.

But there's more. There had been so much hype and PR around that race, about how Snake was the new up-and-comer and that he was going to beat me, plus I was so excited that I had won and that there was going to be a big article about the race in *Drag Racer Magazine*, that I left Half Moon Bay without the money! I was nearly to Los Angeles before I realized that I hadn't been paid!

I turned right around and drove all of the way back to Half Moon Bay and got that money. It was $5,000, and I wasn't going to wait another day to get what rightfully belonged to me.

Don Smith, who was running the event, said as he was handing me the money, "We knew you'd be back."

FUN AND GAMES
WITH THE SNAKE I

Let me tell you something about Don Prudhomme. He is a competitor. He hates to lose. Shirley Muldowney's the same way. And I admire that, because if you don't have that killer instinct, you won't be a champion. Prudhomme has always had it.

Well, we were running each other in the final round of the World Series of Drag Racing in Cordova. Bob Taaffe was my crew chief, and in fact, he was the only help I had. You have to understand that Cordova had a strange setup for the starting lights. The lights actually hung over the starting line, and you had to look up to see them. When you were racing someone, you pulled up until your light turned yellow and then you'd wait for the green to come on. You couldn't see the other guy's light, so you couldn't tell if his yellow was on and he was staged. And you certainly didn't want to look over at his car, because that green could come on at that exact instant and you'd be sitting there.

I was still running Velve-Touch clutches at the time, and when I staged for that final, I had my yellow light on with the engine RPMs up. I was waiting for Snake to pull in, and I didn't dare look over because the light could turn green and he'd be gone. Finally, he pulled in and we got the green, but a piece of my clutch was disintegrating and broke off. It came through the can and

In one of my many match races I had with Don "The Snake" Prudhomme, I beat the Californian at Union Grove in 1972.

burned me something awful on the back of my leg. I still have the scar to this day.

Prudhomme won the race.

FUN AND GAMES WITH THE SNAKE II

Two weeks later, at the Detroit Dragway, wouldn't you know I was running Don Prudhomme again in the final round of a match race. Bob Taaffe was with me again, and he was up at the starting line as we were getting ready to run.

Now, at Detroit they had the same kind of overhead starting light system like Cordova; plus, they had a shield between you and the other guy's light. They just wanted you to get up there, stage, and be ready for the green. They also had a little wall between the lanes, but I could see enough of the other lane to know if the other guy was close to staging.

This time, I wasn't as quick getting staged as I was in Cordova. But I didn't take too much time, either. Out of the corner of my eye, I could see Prudhomme moving up, and he pulled right in. It was a nice, clean start. I outran him this time because I didn't have my clutch building up a lot of extra heat like it did two weeks earlier.

When I got down to the turnoff, I pulled to a stop and saw Prudhomme come around that corner practically on two wheels. He got out of the car, and he was really hot. He said, "I'm gonna kill that son of a bitch when he gets down here! I'm gonna kill him!"

I said, "Snake, Snake, what's wrong?"

He said, "If he ever puts a hand on my car again, I'm gonna to kill him!"

I said, "Snake, calm down, what do you mean?"

He said, "He touched my car! He touched my car when I was staging!"

"Who?"

"Taaffe! Taaffe! I'm gonna kill him!"

Now here comes my truck, and it was coming around the corner on two wheels. Taaffe jumped out of the truck, walked right over to Prudhomme, and said, "Snake, you're going to stage properly from now on."

Snake says, "If you ever touch my car again, I'm gonna kill you!"

Taaffe walked right over to Snake's car, took his fist, and smashed the cowl in. Then he turned around and said to Prudhomme, "I touched your car."

Now Taffe wasn't that big a guy, but he was tough. After he said that to Prudhomme, things began to calm down. I still didn't know what had happened at the starting line, so when Bob and I got into the truck, I asked him, "What the hell happened down there?"

He said, "Well, you remember what happened at Cordova, right?"

I said, "Oh yeah, I remember."

Bob said, "Well, you were staged this time and he was just sitting there not doing anything, and the starter was waving him up to stage and he was still sitting there, so I walked over, grabbed his injector linkage, cranked it up to high-C, and just walked him in."

I said, "Good for you."

That could have been one hellacious fight, but Prudhomme is a cool cat. He soon settled down, he knew he had been wrong, and it never went any further than that. We never had a problem after that whole thing happened. From then on he always raced me straight up and clean.

THE BLOWOVER

By the summer of 1986, Gary Beck's 5.39 was still the quickest time anybody had run. It was a heck of a run, too. We got to Englishtown for the Summernationals with *Swamp Rat XXX*, and we went 5.34 on Friday night. We needed a backup to make it an official record on Saturday, and we knew we could do it.

On my first run on Saturday, I made the burnout, and after I backed up, there was a small drizzle of fuel leaking from the nozzle line on the injectors. Connie Kalitta had spotted it, and he ran over and put his hand in front of my face to hold me up so Herb Parks could try to take care of it. Herb was tightening the fittings and trying to get it to stop, but I was running on full fuel this whole time and the engine was sucking it down. After they determined the leak wasn't that bad, finally, they let me go.

I should have thought it through and realized they had held me too long and I had burned two or three gallons of my fuel. In fact, the car never would have made it to the end on the fuel that was left in it. But Darrell Gwynn, "The Wolf," was in the other lane, and I knew I had him because he had a 5.50 car and I had a 5.30 car. Even though this was qualifying, I wanted to outrun him, back up the record, put another notch in my belt, and say, "I got Gwynn again."

So stupidly, I went up there and staged, not thinking about the possibility of a wheelstand, but I should have been thinking about burning up my engine in the lights if it ran out of fuel. Now, that was the "bull nose" car and it carried 12 gallons of fuel. It was fine-tuned to have just the right amount of weight over the front to keep it balanced during the run. As soon as I hit the throttle, the front wheels came up about four inches. I didn't notice that little bit, but suddenly, the horizon went away. I was somewhere around a 45-degree angle. I still could have done something to keep it under control, and had I pulled back on the brake, it would have come right back down. But I was thinking, "I don't want to do that because I could damage the front end, so I'll just let off the throttle nice and easy and bring it back down gently."

Yeah, riiiiiight!

In an instant, it was flying over. I did grab the brake at that point, but it was too late. And as it was flying up, I'm thinking, "God, I hope none of those safety crews is anywhere near me and I don't hit them." And then I was thinking, "I hope I don't hit anything solid."

I was twirling all around, the cockpit was filling up with smoke, and then suddenly, it stopped. What had happened was I had braced myself for the impact and had stepped back on the throttle, and that spun the tires frontward as I was going backward. It was better than brakes! It stopped in no time.

But now, I was pointed back the other way, the motor was still running and the car was still in gear. That's when the NHRA got scared half to death. They looked up and out of the smoke this Top Fuel dragster was coming right at them, probably with an unconscious driver in it! They were on their radios calling "Mayday! Mayday! Mayday!" They sent one of their crash trucks out to run into my dragster to stop it. It didn't take a rocket scientist to know what they were trying to do. I saw this safety truck heading for me at a pretty good clip, so I turned the car off the track to let them know I was conscious and I wasn't going to let the car get back to the starting line. I knew that if I didn't steer that car off to the side, even if I stopped it, they would have run that truck right into me, and if they did, I would have been hurt much worse than whatever the car might have done to me. That truck would have climbed right over the front wheels of the dragster and come right up to the cockpit.

But what else could they do? This was a runaway dragster as far as they knew.

I got out of the car, and everything turned out OK, but what I should have done was taken the car to a shop and repaired it so I could have been right back out there racing the next day. But I was so happy I didn't hurt anyone or get hurt myself that I didn't run again that weekend and figured I'd rather fix the car in my own shop, on my own chassis jig, and make sure the job was done right.

INDY, 1967

Everybody knows 1967 was the year I promised not to shave off my beard until I ran my first six-second elapsed time, and I finally did it at the U.S. Nationals in Indianapolis. But there's a lot more to that story.

All during the summer of 1967, the Fram Corporation was on the road with me, filming the *Big Daddy Split-Second Showdown*, a 30-minute television show. They wanted the show to end at the U.S. Nationals after following me all summer from here to there, barnstorming, match racing, and going from place to place. They called the NHRA and requested film credentials so they could shoot the finish of the film at Indy.

Frank McGonagle, who was the head of this project for Fram, called the NHRA, and Wally Parks got on the phone with him.

Wally said, "What do you need these film credentials for?"

Frank said, "Well, we're doing this television show on Big Daddy, and the last part of the show is about him racing at the U.S. Nationals."

Wally said, "Ya know, Big Daddy's been around for a long time, but we've got some young drivers coming up who are actually better than him. We've got Don Prudhomme and Tom McEwen and Mike Sorokin. Why don't you do a show on one of them?"

Frank said, "Well, I didn't know that, but we've shot so much film of Big Daddy already that we have to finish the show we had planned or we'll lose a lot of money. Can we have the credentials or not?"

Wally said, "Well, sure, you can have the credentials."

When we got to Indy, we had a rough start. I had the new, experimental Goodyear tires on the car, but this was before they had come out with their really good tires. In the first two runs, we didn't do so well. We were qualified for the 32-car field at No. 23, but we knew we needed some traction to go quicker.

On Monday morning I went over to the M&H trailer and saw Marvin Rifchin and asked him if he had any tires I could buy. He said, "Big Daddy, nothing would make me happier than to sell you a set of tires and get those Goodyears off of there, but I don't have any. James Warren just bought the last set of new tires from me, and I've been watching him. The tires he's been running are pretty good. Maybe he'll sell or loan you his used tires. They'll be just as good as new ones."

So I headed over to see James Warren and told him what I wanted. He said, "Well, I just ran 6.90 with the tires that are on the car, and you can see by the looks of them that they're still pretty good. I actually got the new tires just to have as spares in case something happened. New tires are never as good on the first run anyhow, so why don't you take them and run them in the first round and bring them back?"

I said, "Geez, that's real nice of you, but I don't feel right using your new tires." He said, "No, don't worry about it. They need a run on them, and you probably won't go past the first round anyway."

Nobody else figured I'd go beyond the first round either. However, with good tires, I knew better.

I took those new tires, and as I was rolling them back to my pit, I went past Tom McEwen's pit. He had just set a new national record at 6.76. He said, "Old man, where are you going with those M&H tires?" I said, "I'm going to put them on my car and run in the sixes so I can shave this itchy beard off."

He said, "By the time you run in the sixes, that beard will be snow white and you'll be tripping over it."

Well, I installed the new tires on the car, and in the first round, I raced Jerry Dawson from St. Louis. He had a little bit of a wheelstand, and I got right down there with a 7.10 and beat him. I went back over to James and asked him if he wanted his tires back. He had won his first-round race and had run in the 6.90s, so he wasn't in any hurry to get the new tires back.

In the second round, I had to race "The Hawaiian," the car Roland Leong owned that was driven by Mike Sorokin. Before the run, Roland came over to my pit and said, "Your only hope is that the tires don't smoke."

Sorokin went red and fouled out.

I still hadn't run in the sixes, but I was running in the seven-ohs. I was close.

So the next race was with Tom McEwen. We were in the staging lanes getting ready to run, and in those days, the drivers put their helmets and suits on right there at the car in the lanes and they could talk to one another. It's not like today where the drivers have all of these people around them to help them get into the car and belted in. He and I were sitting in our dragsters, and the last thing McEwen said to me just before he pulled

The most famous instance of personal grooming in drag racing history! I shave at the starting line at Indianapolis Raceway Park in 1967 after winning the U.S. Nationals. I kept my promise to shave if I made a six-second pass. I beat James Warren in the final to do it.

his helmet down over his head was, "Old man, I'm fixin' to give you a driving lesson."

He fouled out.

He turned off early because when he saw his red-light, he just made a little squirt. I went 7.01. So when I was going back past him on the return road, I called to him, "Yeah, that was a good driving lesson. It taught me what not to do!"

So now I had to race Warren in the final. I went over to his pit and said, "I guess now you want your tires back." I had already made arrangements to borrow another set of tires from somebody else. Warren said, "Why would I want my tires back? I just ran 6.91, and you ran 7.01, so obviously, I must have the better tires."

I said, "So I can use them for the finals?"

"Sure," he said, "No problem. Just bring them back after the race."

We went up there, and as I was staging, I pulled way over to the side away from all of that rubber in the center because we were spinning the tires a little bit at the start, and if you had a lot of rubber on the racetrack, you'd spin them. You needed raw pavement.

But it was a good, clean race with no funny business at the starting line, and I beat his 6.85 with a 6.77, only 1/100 of a second off the absolute world record.

It was shaving time.

They pushed me back to the starting line in the car, and after I stopped, I got up on the hood of the truck and at least attempted to shave that beard off. But the fans there stole everything they could get their hands on at the starting line. Every light, every electronic beam, every sensor. They took the Christmas Tree apart— everything was stolen. They even took the wires! So NHRA never let that happen again.

FOUR SECONDS AT OVER 300

The Gwynn team was really very helpful when it came time for me to get my four-second pass and 300 mph speed in *Swamp Rat XXXIV*. I've always been very close to them, and the competitive rivalry that existed between us on the track had nothing to do with our personal relationship.

Swamp Rat XXXIV had been built in 1993, so you can imagine how much updating it needed. I called Jerry Gwynn and told him I really liked the setup that Ken Veney had and asked Jerry whether he minded if I had an exact copy of everything they did. He said, "Not at all." And so I bought what I needed from Ken—the cylinder heads and engine pieces—and started gathering everything together.

The car had a small rear end in it. It was only a nine and a half-inch rear, so I called Bob Stange at Strange Engineering and asked him what he thought. He said, "What is it you want to do?" I told him, "Somewhere around 4.90, maybe 4.88, and 300-plus would be fine."

He said, "You could put a 10 1/2 in there, and that will do it. If you want to go any faster than that, you'll need the big rear end, the 12 1/2-inch unit. The 10 1/2 units are inexpensive. We've got plenty of them, and one of them should do the trick."

That turned out to be a mistake, because we eventually wanted to go faster than that, and we wound up only getting one run on a set of 10.5 gears. That rear end couldn't handle elapsed times in the 4.60s.

This kind of deal is a lot more complicated than you think. Finally, I had to call a nice young man, John Maddox, to help me out. He had worked with the Gwynns and knew the combination. He came down to my shop and spent some time helping me get the car all set up. But there was a lot that had to be done, and I wound up spending a lot of money on this project. We were lucky to get some help from a bunch of people.

But Maddox and I had a falling out. He left some nozzles loose inside the valve cover while we were in Gainesville doing some testing, and the fuel pressure dropped during a run. We burned No. 8 piston, and we had a fire. I wasn't very happy about that.

He just took it like it was just Top Fuel racing and put all of the burned parts aside while reaching for all of the new stuff. Now, we didn't have a lot of parts because all I had wanted to do was go to Indy, make a few runs, not even qualify necessarily, and get my four and my 300 in front of everybody. So I fired him. I shouldn't have done that, because he was a very smart young man and, on top of that, very likeable.

I replenished the parts and went through everything that got damaged. Whatever needed to be fixed, we fixed. I didn't touch all of the new parts, because I wanted to save those for Indy.

We didn't have a crew chief at the time, and we didn't know what we were going to do. It looked like we were going to Indy on our own. Then, a few days before we were going to leave, we got a fax from the NHRA—about 10 or 12 pages—listing everything that needed to be done to the car to bring it up to standards. There wasn't enough time to do it all.

It was 11 o'clock that morning when I walked into the shop and pulled the plug. I had a bunch of guys there working on the car and making parts, but I knew we couldn't make it to Indy.

At about one o'clock that afternoon, the phone rang and it was Gary Clapshaw. Gary said, "My car is entered, and you can drive it." I thought about it for a while, because I was not big on driving other people's cars. But there was so much publicity out there about me wanting to go 300 and, at the same time, everybody was telling me that Gary had a good car, so I finally agreed to it.

When I got to Indy, I couldn't believe what his guys had done. They had put black vinyl over that pretty paint job he had and lettered Matco Tools on it. I'm telling you, the car looked great. You know the rest of the story. I got my 300 and ran 4.72 with a zero, the quickest I had ever been. I never got my cars to go quite that quick.

SWAMP RAT XXXIV

Now, on my four-second run, the car moved around a bit in the middle, just like Shirley Muldowney's car did when I went 287 in it in Dallas and the way Paul Smith's car did at the Autofest 2000. I didn't remember my wing car moving around like that when I tested it in Gainesville and Atlanta; I was convinced I should stay with the project, bring out *Swamp Rat XXXIV*, and see what it would do.

I made the changes on it that the NHRA asked for, and I actually had one of their tech people come up here and look it over. He gave me the OK, and that allowed me to go out and run that 323.04. It wasn't quite as quick, though, because the car was a little too heavy. It came in at about 200 pounds too heavy. Plus, with the rear end that was in it, we shouldn't have tried to go a lot quicker. If we tried to run the car hard enough to run in the 4.50s, we'd have stripped the rear end right out of it. That was the end of *SR-XXIV* in NHRA competition because they outlawed the car as of December 1, 2003, because it was so old.

DON COOK: IRONMAN

Back around 1969, we were at a race up at Union Grove, Wisconsin. Don Cook was racing Don Prudhomme, and after he won, his car had a big explosion. He had all kinds of fire coming back into the car—remember, this was a slingshot car—and he put his arm up in front of his face to shield himself. He wasn't burned because the firesuit protected him, but the suit, especially the right sleeve that shielded his face, got burned up pretty badly.

There was a break rule back then, and if Cook couldn't make it to the next round to race me, Prudhomme would come back in his place. Well, Cook wasn't going to have any of that. There was no way he was going to let Snake get back into the race after he had just beaten him.

Cook was running around the pits and was actually looking to borrow a complete firesuit, but as he was making his way around the pits, he was yelling, "Anyone got a right-hand sleeve for a firesuit? I need a right-hand sleeve for a firesuit!"

Meanwhile, his crew was putting racer's tape over the hole on the side of the oil pan to keep the oil from leaking out from where the rods had come through!

He was coming back to race no matter what! He wasn't going to let the Snake back in, period! And he didn't. Somehow the crew got the car to the starting line.

One time during a race, Cook had something snap by his feet, and it broke his foot. This happened in the middle of the event, and the doctors wanted to take his boot off. Cook said, "No, you can't do that. If you take that boot off, it'll swell right up and you'll never get it back on. We'll take care of the broken foot after the race is over."

And that son of a bitch kept racing all day with that broken foot. He was tough.

YOU WANT TO SEE TOUGH?

We were up at Union Grove, Wisconsin, another time, and this was right after Connie Kalitta and Shirley Muldowney broke up. It was a pretty nasty split, and they had some words between them. So Shirley was pitted a ways across from me, and I saw Connie walking up toward the starting line, staying as close to my side as possible and as far away from hers as he could get. Shirley was sitting in her tow vehicle near the race car, and when Kalitta walked by, she yelled something over at him, some kind of profanity, and he turned around and shouted, "What did you say?" He walked over to where she was and stuck his face into the open window where she was sitting. Suddenly, they were having it out on the spot. Shirley had this young kid helping out on her car, and when he saw what was happening, he picked up a 15-inch breaker bar out of the toolbox, walked over behind Kalitta, and hauled off and hit him in the head! He split Kalitta's head wide open!

Kalitta turned around, looked at this kid holding the breaker bar and said, "You shouldn't have done that." This kid was paralyzed with fear. He just hit a guy with a breaker bar, and that was usually enough to put somebody out cold. The kid didn't even try to get away. Kalitta grabbed the kid by the hair, pulled him toward himself, and hit him with five or six punches until he fell to the ground in a crumpled mess.

Then, Kalitta came over to where I was standing and said, "Take a look at my head and see how bad it is." Well, there was blood pouring down his head and onto his shirt. He was a real mess. I said, "My God, Kalitta, your head is split wide open! You've got to get some stitches!"

He said, "No, no, no…I gotta race! Get some racer's tape!"

So we got some racer's tape and stuck a bunch of it on his head. He pulled the helmet on and down the track he went.

He is one tough man.

BIG DADDY
WAS TOUGH, TOO

I was match-racing at Irwindale one time against Shirley Muldowney. It was the usual "two out of three" format, and after the second race, we had each won one. I was back in the pits, working on the engine, and tightening the head studs up with the torque wrench. But the torque wrench broke. My hand slipped, and I cut one of my fingers off, right through the bone, on the sharp end of a header pipe, and that finger was just hanging off by the skin. Ron Barrow was with me, and I said, "Ron, I've got to get to the hospital right away."

They ran me right over to the hospital while someone went over to Shirley and told her I had cut my finger off. Shirley said, "He's done, that's it."

But it was still pretty early. We had started on time, and there weren't any delays, so there was a good deal of time left. In fact, as I was leaving for the hospital, I told the track people, "Don't run that last round until I get back here."

So they waited. At the hospital, they had me in the emergency room, but nobody was examining me. Finally, I walked down the hallway of the hospital and said, "I need a doctor! I need somebody to sew my finger back on!" A doctor came up to me and said, "We're trying to save your finger!" I said, "You're not doing shit! Nobody's even taken a look at this thing yet! Now, I've got 25,000 people sitting back at the track waiting to see the end of this match race, so would you please sew my finger back on so I can go back and run!"

He was pissed. They had to put wire inside that finger to hold it on and then sew it all together, and they finally put it in a splint so I could get out of there. I got back to the track, cut the finger off of my driving glove so I could get the splint in there, which still gave me fire protection because the splint was plenty thick, and got to the line. Believe it or not, I won the match race!

And she thought I was all done.

We had another match race with Shirley the next day in Fremont. Now, we had to drive all night because it was a Saturday night race in Irwindale and a Sunday afternoon race in Fremont, and by the time we got to Fremont, that finger was throbbing! So I didn't fool around with having to make three runs. I just bit my lip and won the first two. That was it for me, and I went home.

AUTOFEST 2000

In late 1999, a hopeful promoter attempted to gather some of the most famous drag-racing drivers of all time and feature them at a special event at Moroso Motorsports Park in West Palm Beach, Florida, on New Year's Eve. Titled "Autofest 2000," the multi-attraction gala was to offer not only drag racing, but car shows, musical entertainment, and a host of other activities all tied in to the arrival of the new millennium. The highlight of the event was to be a match race between Big Daddy and Shirley Muldowney at midnight, thus having a drag race that spanned both the old and new millennium.

The event was a financial bust and led to bankruptcy proceedings for the unlucky promoter. Many racers have yet to be paid the full amounts they were promised, and some may never receive total payment.

That had to be one of the most bizarre experiences of my life. First of all, the promoter spent money like it was going out of style. He printed up thousands of handouts and had them stuck inside the newspapers, but you know as well as I do, that's the first part of the newspaper you throw away!

He spent a lot of money booking drivers. I heard that he paid Shirley $75,000 to come down and match-race me. He paid Paul Smith $30,000 to provide a Top Fuel car for me to drive, and, of course, he had to pay me, too. That was another $30,000. Some of the money he paid people up front, and some got a portion of the money up front and were supposed to be paid that night.

They had a real hard time attracting people to this race for a couple of reasons. First, it was on the night that the Y2K disaster was supposed to happen, and I can guarantee you there were plenty of people sitting at home, watching the clock tick toward midnight and hoping to God all of the lights didn't go out.

And let me tell you, that whole Y2K hysteria was the biggest farce. Midnight came and went all over the world and nothing happened. It was just a conspiracy to boost the economy by having everyone replace their computers and get new programs. We had a bunch of old computers that we didn't touch, and they still worked just fine after January 1. How many billions of dollars were spent in this country because everyone thought their computers would crash? And yet, in Indonesia and in these poor, primitive countries, nobody had a single problem. But everyone thought this was going to be the end of the world and a lot of people stayed home.

Then, the promoter farmed out the parking contract to this other company for some front-end money. That was a mistake because this company came in and was charging $40 to park! One of the security guards said that half the people who came to the event saw how much the parking was and turned right around and left!

They did get some cars down the racetrack, though. Shirley and I had our match race, at least the first run at midnight, but that almost didn't happen. Smith had gotten $10,000 of the $30,000 he was being paid, but when we were getting ready to make our first run against Shirley, he said, "I'm not running until I get the rest of my money." The promoter got the money and gave it to Paul, and so we ran.

I did my usual match-race procedure and had a soft tune-up in it, figuring I'd have Paul step on it a little for the next run. But Shirley didn't want to run again after she beat me in that first race, so we were through.

But here's the ironic part. Everyone knows I signed off on Shirley's first Top Fuel license back in the 1970s.

Well, I was renewing my Top Fuel license that weekend in West Palm Beach and Shirley signed off on mine.

And one other thing. During my one race with Shirley, as we were running down the track at the stroke of midnight, the lights flickered out for an instant and came back on again.

It was the strangest weekend I think I ever had.